53 Is The
New 38

53 Is The New 38

TALES OF INDIGNITY AND MIDDLE AGE

Michael Anthony Turpin

ISBN: 1517093694
ISBN 13: 9781517093693

Dedication

To My Friend and Life Sponsor, Lloyd Aubrey: I never would have made it to fifty without you

Men do change, and change comes like a little wind that ruffles the curtains at dawn, and it comes like the stealthy perfume of wildflowers hidden in the grass.

John Steinbeck

Men are like parking spaces: The good ones are taken and the only ones left are handicapped.

Anonymous

From Russia with Love

*"The Cold War isn't thawing; it is burning with a
deadly heat. Communism isn't sleeping; it is, as
always, plotting, scheming, working, fighting."*
—RICHARD M. NIXON

I N THE SUMMER of 1971, I saw the movie *Dr. Strangelove or: How I Learned to
Stop Worrying and Love the Bomb*. At ten years old, I did not totally appreciate bizarre characters like Brigadier General Jack D. Ripper or Dr. Strangelove.
I could not entirely understand why Slim Pickens, aka Major T.J. "King" Kong,
rode the atomic bomb out of the B-52 bomber like a bucking bronco. However,
I clearly understood that the United States and the Soviet Union were fighting
a cold war.

My fiery imagination was stoked by a father who was constantly criticiz-
ing the country for letting down our guard against commies, pinkos and spies.
Hollywood was full of Reds, and while Senator Joseph McCarthy did his best in
the '50s to root out these ideological weeds, communist dogma was invasive
and required relentless vigilance to detect and remove political parasites. The
entertainment industry, Congress, all of Europe, and even our church had been
infiltrated by the vodka-swilling, plate-breaking, Gulag-operating, godless col-
lectivists who were just biding their time waiting for the last capitalist to sell
them the rope they would hang us with.

I had to do my patriotic duty and keep our neighborhood safe for democracy. This task required me to develop a clandestine intelligence organization to inform on any person who might be providing secrets to the enemy. One never knew where a sleeper cell might be cocooned. Authors like Robert Ludlum described how agents could lie dormant for a generation. A Manchurian candidate could be activated with a simple phone call.

"Is this Mrs. Ruth Turpin of 1828 Windsor Road?"

"Yes. Who is this?"

"Sasha sells sea shells by the sea shore."

Hearing this heavily accented, tongue-twisting alliteration, my mother, the sleeper agent, would go into a brainwashed trance, drive her station wagon up the winding mountain roads of Mount Wilson and blow up the radio tower, disabling all radio and TV transmissions across the San Gabriel Valley and isolating us from the outside world.

Just up the street in Pasadena was Caltech, a bastion of high-IQ engineers, rocket scientists, and astrophysicists. We were a tempting target. The 64,000-ruble question was which of my neighbors actually might be conspiring to sabotage our town. Could the confederate turn out to be someone we never suspected, like green-thumbed Mr. S, who upon being activated would fly across the country to Washington, D.C., and attempt to assassinate President Nixon with his trowel? Spies were clever and not easy to catch. They were ruthless and not above posing as retirees, gardeners, and even parents.

I recruited my friends to assist me in watching our neighborhood. Of particular interest was Mr. H, who lived across the street with his parents and kept odd hours. We also had some concerns about Mr. M, who routinely screamed at us to get off his lawn. Vodka and socialism made people angry and loud. Perhaps Mr. M missed the snows of Moscow and was annoyed at the constant sun and temperate climate of Southern California.

On a warm summer afternoon, armed with binoculars, a Polaroid camera, and walkie-talkies, we embarked on a series of information-gathering patrols. The next morning, my mother received several angry calls from neighbors who were concerned over a disturbed child peering into windows, crawling through juniper bushes, and in one case taking a photograph.

Although I was not identified in person, the default accusation on our block was to always blame the Turpin boys. Annoyed and lacking actionable information, my mother could not deduce the identity of the young peeping Tom. As all good spies do, I lied convincingly when interrogated. I even provided an alibi. While she could not prove anything, she lectured me about people's personal privacy. If she only knew that we had already uncovered some seamy information about some of our upstanding fellow citizens, including the disgusting fact that one ultra-tan neighbor sunbathed in the nude and mowed his back yard in a Speedo while craven neighborhood women watched him from their adjacent upstairs windows. Moral decline was omnipresent.

My parents were naïve and did not understand that the town was teeming with traitors. I even suspected my brother of selling information to foreign agents. He was a weak individual with liberal ideas. I searched his room and discovered a magazine stuffed between his mattresses. It was called, amazingly, *From Russia with Love* and had a beautiful woman in a provocative pose on the cover. It was obviously intended for fans of the 1963 James Bond thriller starring Sean Connery.

The magazine was weathered and torn. I opened it, and to my delight and shame, I saw photographs of naked "Russian" women. None of these women were as sinister as SMERSH/SPECTRE agent Rosa Klebb, the spy who attempted to kill James Bond with a poison-tipped knife that jutted out from the end of her boot. No, these women seemed...well...more open to détente.

As any dedicated spy would, I immediately disappeared behind the garage to study the magazine so that if I ever saw any of these women in public, I could identify them even with their clothes on.

After committing each page to memory, I carefully tucked the magazine under my pillow and went off to school, ready to share what I had learned with my confederates in Mr. Stebbins' gym class. I knew my brother would not report the magazine missing. Yet, as fate would have it, while I was sitting through Social Studies class, my mother was making my bed.

I rode home in record time, as I was eager to examine the magazine models for other distinguishing features. As I walked in the back door, I immediately knew something was not right. My smirking brother escorted me into the dining room, which was the center for all interrogation and corrective action. My mother appeared overly concerned, and for a moment I thought there had been a death in the family.

"Honey," she said, "is there anything you want to talk to me or your dad about?" I was stumped and then I saw the magazine on the chair next to her. "That's not mine," I protested. "It's Tom's!"

"The neighbors have been complaining about someone peeking in their windows, and now I have found this adult magazine in your room. I think you and your dad need to have a talk."

Suddenly it hit me. I had been framed. I was obviously getting too close to someone or something and they wanted me out of the way. As my dad always said, those Reds were a determined foe and would go to great lengths to expunge any threat. Later that evening I endured my father's unimaginative and anatomically confusing homily on the birds and the bees. I already had heard a more graphic and entertaining version from my friend Dennis Higgins in gym class. It would do me no good to attempt an explanation to my dad. I would have to endure this punishment and bide my time.

One thing was certain. When I got older, I wanted to join the CIA, especially if it meant interrogating one of those Russian women. After all, I was probably the only guy who could pick them out of a line-up.

Cock-a-Doodle Doo-Doo

"Uniqueness is the commodity of glut."
—MATT RIDLEY, GENOME

IN THE ANCIENT animal kingdom of my youth, there were only two kinds of dogs: mongrels and pedigrees. Purebred dogs dominated film and television, as canines such Lassie and her Aryan cousin, the German shepherd Rin Tin Tin proved time and again that the pedigreed dog was indeed man's best friend.

The mongrel, however, was viewed as a poor relation and a mere supporting actor. With names like Tiger and Scout, these mud-bloods were furry accessories and semi-domesticated symbols of the nuclear family.

They greeted us on our front door steps, would willingly eat broccoli passed under the table, slept in doghouses, and protected personal property across America's rural and suburban communities. Mongrel dogs were a microcosm of our nation—a melting pot whose murky mélange of genetics produced a strange but strong alloy.

Veterinarians were trained in school to use more politically correct clinical terms such as "pound puppy" or "mixed breed" to describe a dog with questionable heritage. Our vet explained that our mixed-breed dog was smart and resourceful, a testimony to his confused lineage and hard-knocks upbringing. Max was a poodle, shepherd, and terrier mix. It must have been quite a party the night he was conceived. His genetic cards left him looking like the lead guitarist in an acid rock band—wild, matted hair; crazed eyes; and an inability to focus. He was a fearless guard dog with the guts of a burglar and a pit bull's resolve. He would chase anything that moved, including cats, trash men, small children, and trucks—the last of which eventually bested him.

Our neighbors, on the other hand, had a purebred Dalmatian, a dog more tightly wound than the lug nuts on a new bridge. Luigi had managed to bite every kid in our town, earning a rap sheet his owner felt was undeserved. In the epoch of Jurassic parenting, when children always were considered guilty until proven innocent, a kid might come home crying of a dog bite and immediately be interrogated by an angry adult: "Well, what the hell did you do to make Luigi bite your arm?" In those days, the benefit of the doubt always fell to the Kennel Club canine with papers.

Around the block was another purebred—a German shepherd named Lobo who was probably more inbred than the descendants of the *Bounty* on Pitcairn Island. Lobo had bad hips and could not catch an 80-year-old with a walker. However, he was crafty. He would crouch by a low retaining wall, waiting patiently for kids walking home from school before he thrust his front legs onto the wall and lunged at us, savagely barking. His owner, Mr. Silbernagel, would yell at us while his dog threatened to turn us into eunuchs. "Hey, you kids, quit teasing that animal."

Germans loved their purebreds. Yet most of their breeds—Doberman pinschers, shepherds, and mastiffs—were bred primarily for law enforcement or personal property protection. Even my grandparent's schnauzer, Flossie, had a chip on her shoulder. The only exception to this Aryan purebred factory of fierce creatures was the dachshund, which was really France's idea of a funny birthday present to the Kaiser who liked Wiener Schnitzel. As usual, the Germans failed to see the humor and a few weeks later invaded Metz.

As an adult, I finally confronted my sense of inferiority for never having owned a purebred and purchased an Australian shepherd. I had always been fascinated with working dogs—border collies, Aussies, and Queensland heelers. Brody, the tricolor Aussie herder, was our first effort to join the elite circle of pedigree owners. As I drove to the dog park with Brody, I felt a strange mixture of pride and betrayal. Somewhere in the cosmos, Max The Mongrel was lifting his leg on me for selling him out. Turning into Spencer's Run dog park, I spied a United Nations of breeds intermingling, chasing, tumbling, and pouncing.

Brody's genetic programming kicked in within a minute of being in the park. He wanted to go to work. The area was imploding with happy anarchy, and he was determined to restore law and order. I suddenly heard the dreaded four-word query that would plague me for months to come. I scanned the yard for Brody and watched as he stood victorious over a Weimaraner. The incensed owner pointed at Brody and screamed, "Whose dog is this?"

Minutes later I was skulking out of the dog park like a drunk thrown out of a German beer hall during Oktoberfest. It's actually hard to get tossed from either a dog park or a German bar in October. But Brody had out worn our welcome. As I dragged my happy but bewildered buddy to the car, a woman walked by with a microscopic caramel-colored short-haired dog with massive ET eyes, alert ears, and perfect hypoallergenic hair.

"What kind of dog is he?" I asked.

She surveyed me and my Aussie as if we were immigrant convicts fresh off the ship at Ellis Island. "Francine is a triple chi-mini-poo."

"Isn't that a drink at Starbucks?" I asked.

"She is three parts Chihuahua, one part miniature pinscher, and one part cockapoo. She never sheds, understands Spanish and English, and has one bowel movement a day that is the size of a peanut."

I suddenly pondered Brody's relentless regularity; his matted hair that required constant brushing, and felt woefully inadequate, as if my leaping, twisting, enthusiastic herder were an outdated version of a Calloway driver.

"Let's go home, Buddy. I need to read some Tolstoy to you tonight." I walked away dejectedly and then remembered the woman's condescending look. "You know, on second thought, let's go back into that dog park and make some trouble for these mutants."

As we reentered doggie dystopia, I became aware of the weird and subtle genetic nuances in many of these dogs. They were not just labs, spaniels, cockapoos and terriers; they were genetically modified vegetables. An animal scurried by my feet and I jumped. It resembled a New York City roof rat more than a dog. It ran past me and jumped into the arms of its owner. The man cooed to the dog-rat saying, "Good boy, Cujo." I wondered if Cujo slept on a bed or in a hamster cage.

I could not help eavesdropping on two Millennial Mendels as they described their genetically altered companions. "Ginger is a ChiShihTzuNot—a Chihuahua shih tzu mix with a Nottingham terrier. She's not like that BullShihtz over there." She pointed to what looked like a miniature bulldog wearing a curly brown hair shirt. "The bull breeds are so mischievous and unreliable. Ginger is very consistent. If she scratches at the door, she really does need to go outside to use the rest room. This breed is all business."

Brody ran off as he spotted an English Springer Spaniel racing along the fence line. I could almost see his brain calculating the angle that would assure him the shortest distance to intercept the moving object. As he bolted, I whistled at him to stop. It was no good; his genetics were firmly in control, and it was looking as if I would be once again be kicked out of the dog park.

In a flash, he closed the distance on his prey and lowered his head, ready for a spectacular takedown. As I winced and cringed, the spaniel miraculously sprouted two small flaps and lifted itself in the air as Brody crashed into the railing and tumbled head over heels. The spaniel fluttered harmlessly to the ground and continued on his run. Brody looked like a cold-cocked fighter, staggering back to me and collapsing at my feet.

A young man leaned over and smiled. "Pretty cool, huh? He's one of those Turkey BoxSprings—a cross between a Springer, boxer, and turkey vulture. Apparently, they are one hell of a dog. They even eat roadkill. Don't you just dig his weird little wings?"

I shook my head and then noticed one dog walking with determined conviction, his left side to the fence. He patrolled with serious intensity, never leaving the park's perimeter. He had the head of a mastiff, the wrinkled chrome-blue folds of a shar pei and the musculature of a bulldog. He looked powerful, but clearly was uncomfortable mingling with the mixed breeds.

"So what kind of dog is that?" I asked pointing at the tough solitary creature.

The young man looked up and shook his head. "Newt? He's always here. He's a strange mix between a Neapolitan mastiff and a Conroy pit bull. It's an odd breed. He's very tough but never leaves the right side of the fence. Don't approach him from the left. He lacks peripheral vision and he might bite you."

"What the heck do you call a breed like that?"

He smiled and replied as he walked away, "I think they call him a NeoCon."

Odontophobe

*"I told my dentist I had yellow teeth. He
told me to buy a brown tie."*
—RODNEY DANGERFIELD

I HAVE CERTAIN nightmares that recur with bizarre frequency. Stress, tight deadlines, or being asked to pick up dog poop in the garden can trigger the same dream: I awaken back in college, minutes before all my final exams, and I have not attended a class all semester. To my father's chagrin, this dream is not too far from what actually happened during my sophomore year, but the nightmare is nevertheless unnerving at 53 years old.

A rarer nocturnal gem arrives without warning and involves having my teeth literally falling out as I am eating or speaking. I am certain this relates to my lifelong phobia about going to the dentist. This irrational fear plagues most people except masochists and hillbillies and certainly was a burden carried by our ancestors. Ancient dentistry was at best, primitive. If necessary, the farrier/cobbler/dentist could—and would—use the same rasp to file a hoof and then extract your aching bicuspid. Medieval dentists might yank anything that appeared even to be thinking about decay. Decay, whether moral or oral, was to be rooted out. The pain was a character-building penance.

April, 1968. The blue postcard arrived in the mail like the sinister letter filled with orange seeds in the Sherlock Holmes story "The Five Orange Pips." It was a death notice. My reaction was akin to the five phases of grief: anger, denial, bargaining, depression, and finally a grudging acceptance, usually all within about twelve minutes. The author of the invitation from the House of Pain was Dr. Allen, our dentist and a certain descendent of the Marquis de Sade.

Our dentist sported an army crew cut and looked like an evil ventriloquist—grinning and flirting with our mother while saying under his breath, "You may feel a *little* sting." This Dr. Jekyll would paternally put his arm around me and lead me into the dungeon while my mom sat down to her *Redbook*. Once I was trapped in the chair, Dr. Jekyll became Mr. Hyde, DDS.

X-rays were taken by jamming a T-shaped piece of reinforced white cardboard the size of a shoetree into my cheek, which caused immediate pain and involuntary tearing. Then Dr. Allen probed my teeth with a sharp, pointed instrument to see if he could make me leap to the ceiling. A mark on the wall presumably indicated the record for the highest jump once a nerve had been hit. It was held by a fourth grader from Alhambra. If he found an actual cavity, he acted as if he had caught me stealing money from the orphans' fund at church.

The fear and loathing blossomed into full-fledged terror just prior to the cavity's being filled. "You know, Cindy," Dr. Allen would say, "I don't think we need any Novocain. It's a small cavity."

At this point, my eyes would bug out of my head like a cartoon and I would furiously tap an SOS with my hand, hoping my mother could understand Morse code. I had no voice; my mouth was full of cotton and my throat dryer than an Arizona riverbed in July.

"Almoooost done," he would say inattentively, dismissing my protests and shooting a wink at the lithe, delectable Cindy, his 25-year-old hygienist, who seemed very fit but was clearly not the sharpest instrument on Dr. Allen's tray.

The dental turmoil train just kept chugging along when in young adulthood I was told my wisdom teeth needed to come out. My oral surgeon did not feel general anesthetic was required, so he instead shot me up with a quart of Novocain. At this point my eyes were frozen in place. I could only stare, dead from the neck up. He clamped my back teeth and literally put his knee on my chest as he yanked out and broke off each of my four wisdom teeth.

Suffering from post-extraction trauma disorder, I decided to boycott the dentist for several years. This proved to be a bad idea. The day of reckoning resulted in five cavities and a root canal. I chose a New Age, roller-blading, Deadhead dentist with a ponytail, who gave me headphones to wear during the drilling and enough anesthetic to numb every beaver in North America. Yes, it was an expensive lesson, but I was relieved that dentistry had advanced since the Dark Ages of Dr. Allen.

What a difference a few years can make. My kids actually look forward to the dentist. Their pitted teeth are treated with the equivalent of Kevlar to prevent any plaque attack. They can eat sugar. Today's pediatric dentists are child psychologists and pain-free practitioners. *Where the heck was I?* I thought, when my son needed emergency dental work after cracking his eyeteeth engaging in what my father regularly referred to as "grab ass."

The dental office had flat screens with headphones piping in Nickelodeon cartoons in front of each chair and what seemed like twelve hygienists: one to wipe my son's nose, another to hold his hand, and a third to tell the pediatric dentist what fine work he was delivering to this very lucky boy. It seemed unfair. Where were the leather strap and the glowing, red-hot knife to dig out his broken tooth?

I have to admit it is easier for me as well. Nowadays, my friend and painless partner, Dr. Bill Fessler, plays mood music while his compassionate hygienists regularly coax me back into his dental chair. He is a die-hard Fighting Irish fan and a wonderful blend of psychologist, counselor, and physician. We have an implied non-disclosure agreement ensuring that no one will ever know that I still whine like a four-year-old.

On one particular visit, he asked me if I had ever worn braces. Given that my use-it-or-lose-it flexible spending account was overfunded, I decided to take the plunge and opt for adult braces. A day after being fitted with my new acrylic tracks by a pediatric orthodontist, I happened upon a group of my son's 12-year-old friends and lamented my recent dental work. I received understanding nods and sympathy. Everyone in this posse of prepubescent brace faces accepted me as an honorary member of the zipper-mouth gang.

"Mr. T, don't kiss any girls with braces!"

Another piped up, "Oh yeah, be sure to check the mirror because gross junk will be stuck in your teeth all the time. You can use your phone's selfie screen to check your face. No Tootsie Rolls, Airheads, gum, or salt water taffy."

"Got it," I said, "especially about the kissing the girls with braces."

That night, I had a Kafkaesque nightmare in which I was transforming into a horse with huge eyeeteeth, sort of like old Lampwick when he goes to Pleasure Island with Pinocchio. Intellectually, I was completely prepared for the braces. Emotionally, my tongue and lips kept sending my brain signals that the Eiffel Tower had been constructed inside my mouth. Somewhere in a prison for the criminally insane, Dr. Allen was laughing.

Aside from the sensation that a Metro North commuter train was cutting across my gums, life marched on. I mumbled more, smiled less, and vainly try to perfect a laugh that completely disguised my tin grin. It was a lot of work and a humbling exercise in vanity. Eight months later, I was relieved of my translucent grill and experienced my first Hollywood smile. It looked good. I was still pudgy and middle-aged but the choppers were looking fine. My maintenance kit came with plastic mouth guards that I had to wear each night to keep my ivories in place. I had not informed my dentist that maintenance was not one of my strong suits. Three years later, the nighttime mouth guards had been lost or left in one of a dozen hotel bathrooms. My teeth are now regressing along with every other part of my body.

I recently visited Dr. Bill and met his friendly new hygienist. As I lay on my back enduring her gentle probes, she queried me in a muffled, matter-of-fact voice. "Have you ever thought about braces?"

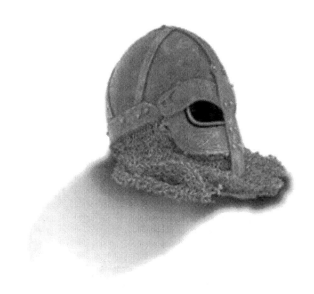

Walk It Off

"Pain is weakness leaving the body."
—Tom Sobal

IN 1000 AD England, King Ethelred the Unready was supreme ruler of Britain. For everyone—royalty and peasants alike—life was a gossamer strand that could be snapped by a sudden invisible hand as easily as one might brush aside a spider's web.

Healers relied on sacred and profane remedies to exorcise the physical demons that brought plagues and misery. In darker times, giving in meant giving up. People learned early to chide and cajole the injured and infirm ("Gettest thou out of bed. Thou still hast breath in thy body!), as if acknowledging the severity of their condition would result in a self-fulfilling prophecy.

In the late 1500s, an unusual illustrated journal maintained by an eleventh-century monk revealed much about life and death in the Dark Ages. One protracted pictograph of medieval medicine shows leeches being applied to the legs of individuals with circulatory and psychological ailments. With their parasitic poultices in tow, the afflicted were expected to walk great distances, presumably to increase circulation, which in turn swelled the growth of the leech until it literally burst off the patient's skin. This bloody explosion was said to mark the point at which the bad blood had been extracted, improving the odds for a speedy recovery. It was theorized by one etymologist that this was the genesis of the Anglican stiff-upper-lip expression "Walk it off."

Now, centuries later, I still recall being beaned in the right leg by Jim Gott, an all-county pitcher who threw laser fastballs in excess of ninety miles per hour. Gott went on to enjoy a decade-long career in Major League Baseball, with stints as a reliever for the Blue Jays, Giants, and Dodgers. On this day, however, during a scrimmage, he all but fractured my femur with a low, tight slider that chose not to break. I still remember the blinding flash of pain and the taste of red dirt on my tongue as I writhed in the chalk of the batter's box. I also distinctly recollect the unsympathetic cacophony of fathers and coaches who all yelled out at precisely the same moment, "Walk it off, Turpin!"

As I got up, limping, I glared though the chain-link backstop. I saw disdain on the ancient faces of the onlookers and could almost divine their prehistoric thoughts: "That kid! What a milquetoast!" and "It's just as well his father isn't here to see this."

Injuries were common in the era of free-range kids. There were road-rash bicycle accidents, sandlot-football broken arms, Fourth of July firework burns, and new-scout-knife gashes. We knew emergency room nurses by their first names. Yet these ladies saw only a fraction of our maladies, because, like most families of our generation, we used the "O-Cubed" method to triage medical events. The O-Cubed rule stated that one must be bleeding from at least three orifices to merit professional medical attention.

This therapeutic best practice was not unique to our family. It was an indispensable axiom for our entire neighborhood, including the Del Santo family, a classically prolific, 12-kid Italian Catholic family whose house was on the diagonal to our back yard.

The Dels' kitchen was a 24-hour MASH unit. I can distinctly recall one of the Del Santo boys dislocating his finger and attempting to get treatment from Mrs. Del, a saint of a mother who, while holding a screaming baby, cooking bacon and eggs, and dragging around two other toddlers who appeared to be attached to her ankles, adroitly administered a field dressing with the detached calm of a battlefield corpsman.

In a treatment torn from the pages of a survivalist field manual, Mrs. Del grabbed a long plastic Lego and scotch tape, and set the finger. Both patient and parent seemed content with the makeshift splint, although I was stunned that the stopgap remedy became permanent and was never replaced with the popular metal splint encased in white gauze and athletic tape.

In the days of "man up" medicine, athletic coaches did not get sued for pushing athletes to the point of heat exhaustion or vomiting. Having survived the army with a crusty master sergeant who was the only survivor of a platoon overrun in North Korea, my father considered pain an essential process in forging stronger character. Through suffering, one could achieve a higher plane of consciousness where pain ultimately subsided (we now know that this higher plane is called shock). However, in the tough-it-out and shake-it-off days, no one iced a monkey bump the size of a golf ball, paid attention to the bruise that resembled the continent of Australia on a kid's left quad, or woke up a Pop Warner football player every hour after he took a shot to the head.

It was not uncommon for a Turpin boy to come into the house bawling uncontrollably after he had pounded a nail through his hand while building a primitive fort or plunged an ice pick into his thigh while removing grout from the shower. Parents of the '60s would actually hit kids to calm them down, perhaps influenced by war movies where the tough officer slaps the hysterical wounded man: "Get hold of yourself, Bob! You still have your other leg." Once the child was slapped out of self-pity, the parent would pour stinging rubbing alcohol on the gaping wound, causing the patient to shriek and jump out of the chair. Another therapeutic slap reduced the child to a drooling, blubbering, shaking mass of bloodstained clothes.

In days before the over-prescription of antibiotics created superbugs and killer staph infections, a boil would not be considered life threatening but instead would be lanced with a sterilized sewing needle and protected with a simple three-inch Band-Aid. A summer splinter was dug out with that same needle.

One would think that this tough-love regimen would have produced a society of practical homeopaths who eschewed formal medicine for Krazy Glue and anti-bacterial ointment. However, as we became parents, we transformed from Darwinian fatalists into empathetic, hyperactive helicopter parents. At every sniffle, sneeze, or throaty cough, we rushed our first-borns to emergency clinics and pediatricians, begging for antibiotics because we could not stand the uncertainty of an illness.

As we got older, had more kids, and realized our children were more or less indestructible objects, we became part of the cavalcade of walk-it-off parents. After our son fell while swinging on his pull-up bar, we chastised him and sent him to bed despite his complaints that his hand was hurting. Two days later, he was diagnosed with a broken bone in that hand (okay, so maybe it was four days later).

Our daughter took a bad spill while playing soccer and again there was whining about a sore shoulder and neck. "You're fine," we told her as she complained about being too sore to practice. Three days after the injury, we stared, abashed, at the X-ray that revealed the broken collarbone. These may have been our finest walk-it-off moments.

It is a cool autumn football night as I wander over to midweek practice fields that buzz under an eerie glow reminiscent of alien landing lights. A symphony of yells, whistles, smacking helmets, and tribal clapping is followed by a singular outburst: "Break!"

A padded adolescent warrior lies on the ground and is slow getting up. As players take a knee in a sign of solidarity, a coach sympathetically touches the player's shoulder pad and coaxes him to sit up. Across the turf field, a father paces uneasily. His large build and slight limp suggest a lifetime of contact athletics. He is barely restraining his need to run on to the field to grab his son. He moves closer to the sideline, straining to see his player and attempting to ascertain the nature of his injury. As a veteran tough-it-out parent, I move toward him to reassure him that his progeny will be fine. But he can hold it in no longer. Cupping his hands to his mouth, he screams, "Come on, Jimmy. You're fine. Get back in there!"

I feel a sudden chill and for a moment sense my father right behind me, seated on wooden bleachers, urging me to suck it up and get back in the game. I turn, expecting to see him restlessly pacing, waiting for me to dust myself off and hustle down to first base.

There is no one there. As I return to my observation post, I stumble over an equipment bag tossed on the sidelines and twist my knee on the turf. Dusting myself off and limping over to the fence, I glance up, hoping no one has witnessed my gaffe. In the shadows lurks another alumnus of the suck-it-up academy.

"Walk it off, dude" he says with a chuckle.

dysfunctional
birthday crown

Birthdaze

"I don't pay attention to the number of birthdays. It's weird when I say I'm 53. It just is crazy that I'm 53. I think I'm very immature. I feel like a kid. That's why my back goes out all the time, because I completely forget I can't do certain things anymore—like doing the plank for 10 minutes."

—ELLEN DEGENERES

O N MY THIRTEENTH birthday, parties and multiple presents ceased. My father slipped out the back door for work as he did each morning. My mother mentioned that my birthday dinner of hamburgers would be warming in the oven when I got home from football practice, as she and my father were out entertaining clients that evening. Clearly, I was no longer the cute puppy worthy of special attention.

I stared at the ground not wanting to cry; I secretly wished that stigmata would appear on my palms to reveal my deep spiritual martyrdom. My only birthday present, a baseball glove, had been purchased weeks before and immediately put to use. My only other gift was a bizarre offering from my grandfather, who clearly was one April away from being able to hide his own Easter eggs. Instead of my annual birthday card accompanied by a crisp ten-dollar bill, I received a coffee can full of pennies and peppermints.

That night, I surveyed the wreckage of my birthday and considered the present value of my waning childhood—pennies, mints, and a shriveled burger on a stale bun. My older brother sensed my dejection and confirmed my worst fears: "Dude, birthdays are over."

Denial became anger. My friend Gary was having his bar mitzvah. I wasn't even sure what this ancient rite of passage entailed, but I heard it meant money, presents, cake, and an excuse to invite girls to a party.

Now I wanted to be Jewish. Gary would be carried in a chair as everyone celebrated that he had become a man. People would stuff money in his trousers like a Chippendale's dancer. He might even grow a beard right then and there from the sheer testosterone of so many acknowledging his manhood.

And here I sat, the Protestant nobody, eating a stale burger and counting out $3.23 in pennies that smelled like Maxwell House. It was my first realization that the grand celebrations of my natal anniversary would now to be castrated and marginalized. Someone needed to inform me just how I was supposed to celebrate an adult birthday.

They should have started by sharing that in the post-pubescent teenage years, each birthday is an event in two phases: a perfunctory family celebration, endured like a morning in church, followed by a private "bash." In the lexicon of the '70s, a successful birthday bash was defined as an event with no adult supervision, limited police intervention, and no one getting sick in your car.

In your twenties, the festivities involved an evening out with everyone, and I mean everyone—friends, coworkers, and that Romanian immigrant busboy you just met at the wine bar in Century City. Birthdays were both a justification for self-indulgence and life lessons.

The "I made it" mentality kicked in and you sought to reward yourself. This led to an extension course at the school of hard knocks as the celebration could take a bizarre turn, resulting in your waking up the next day with a fat lip, no idea where you parked, and a thousand-dollar wad of your VISA receipts signed by someone named Little Ray.

In your thirties and forties, you celebrate your birth anniversary with the parents of your children's friends who have become your friends. You realize your social circle is now completely composed of those who live in your dimension. Their unwavering companionship is your gift. They offer you understanding and never question why your foxhole smells the way it does. Their foxhole is in the same shape. You dream of the perfect adult birthday present: zero accountability to anyone for twenty-four hours—a time everybody just leaves you alone. All you want is to sleep in, work out, play a little golf, and maybe get a massage or haircut. You want to eat something unhealthy, watch your favorites on TV, and not be told to change the channel, wash a dish, pick up a kid, or move a trashcan.

In your fifties, you begin to dread birthdays like the snap of a latex glove preceding a prostate exam: "This may feel a little uncomfortable." You mourn the passing of each year and consider celebrating the day of your birth tantamount to dancing on your own grave. Some regress, anxiously looking into their life's rear view mirror and taking an inventory of all their regrets. The day becomes a black Sabbath of angst and meaningless self-pity. These thoughts may culminate in the rash purchase of a sports car or, worse yet, running off with your personal trainer (Porsche and Viagra ads actively target these unfortunates). However, you probably avoid these irrational impulses and begin to pay homage only to birthdates divisible by five. You use the in-between birthdays as justification for binging on Ben & Jerry's.

As you get on in years, you appreciate every birthday you're granted but prefer celebrating in privacy or perhaps a quiet dinner with another couple or anyone older than you. You buy all your own birthday presents because you are no longer willing to be gracious. You eventually get to a point where you don't want to see anyone, including yourself, in the mirror. A great birthday is simply a day when all your body parts obey.

Birthdays follow a cunning symmetry. As an infant and young child, your first ones find you wetting your pants and rubbing cake all over your face while unfamiliar people crowd around you and take photos. You really haven't a clue about what's happening or why that fat woman with the blue hair keeps pinching your cheek. You get angry when someone you don't know sits next to you: that seat was reserved for your imaginary friend.

Eighty years later, life comes full circle and you're once again wetting your pants, wondering what's going on, and missing your mouth by a country mile as you drop your cake onto the floor. You still get angry when someone sits next to you as you tell everyone repeatedly that *this* seat is reserved for George Clooney. They don't listen, so you hurl your cake and it just happens to hit your stuck-up daughter-in-law in the face; she runs from the room crying, claiming after all these years you still hate her.

Now *that* is a great birthday.

Mater ex Machina

"A mother is a person who seeing there are only four pieces of pie for five people, promptly announces she never did care for pie."
—TENNEVA JORDAN

*I*N ANCIENT TIMES, *Greek and Roman plays would incorporate chaotic twists and turns resulting in situations so entangled that only a god or goddess, literally descending amongst the quarrelling mortals via a basket or rope, could reconcile the temporal knots, bringing order and a timely but highly improbable resolution. The term to describe this miraculous intervention is Deus ex machina: God from the machine.*

My widely dispersed family of origin now gathers primarily for weddings, funerals, anniversaries, and medical crises. On these rare occasions, we reconnect through storytelling, usually at the expense of our father. Each son arrives with his own mental shoebox full of family mythology and proceeds to look for opportune times to mischievously recount a story. My dad, aka T-Rex, takes it well but at times contests our version of the "Brussel Sprout Affair" or debates the actual percentage of our wages he garnished for punishments.

Although my mother's loud laugh and tireless energy have been depleted by Parkinson's disease, she listens intently as we gather to dredge the river of our lives. Her eyes still flash bright, opalescent blue when we recount the myriad stories that have become threads in a raucous and irreverent family tapestry.

My mother was made to bring up boys. She used candor, insight, and trust to soften and shape the well-intended but clueless scrum of men she birthed one after the other. She had a sixth sense about people and would often encourage us to "use your antennas to read people and situations. Everyone's antenna is different, with some people, like your father, picking up only major signals. Others, like short-wave-radio operators, pick up multiple signals, making them both intuitive and easily distracted."

Her intuition proved an invaluable asset to my father in business and in life. She could anticipate situations, read people, and disarm stuffy customers with her humor and alarming honesty. She longed for a daughter but resigned herself to the fact that her life would be a world filled with dirty toilet seats, sweaty clothes, and GI Joes. She waited patiently for the day that her sons might bring home girlfriends and wives—girls who later would be alarmed by how much these boys confided in their mother.

In *A Few Good Men*, Jack Nicholson screams at Tom Cruise, "You want the truth? You can't handle the truth!" My father was an advertising executive from a generation whose marital trousseau was limited to a high IQ, bachelor's degree and strong work ethic. He worked countless hours driven by the four financing horseman of fear: college tuition, orthodontia, the mortgage, and the family cars. That left my mother to serve as teacher, confessor, and staff sergeant of a five-man testosterone army. She *could* handle the truth.

Her army knew the basic rules:

1) Transparency...or "If I hear it from you first, the punishment will be only half as bad." Her tell-me-everything approach worked as a catharsis for guilty minds and was its own form of therapy. This first rule resulted in a scene repeated many times: a Turpin boy racing home, desperate to beat a patrol car or a neighbor's incriminating phone call. We referred to my mom as "sodium pentothal," because she could coax the darkest truth out of the most estranged individual.

2) Discretion...or "I'll decide what to tell your father." Given The T-Rex's limited bandwidth in dealing with much beyond job and family obligations, my mother would not burden him with all the daily infractions and near-death experiences that occurred. She is only now breaking to him things that happened to me in 1982.

3) Broadmindedness...or "I want you to be open to new things." While my dad escorted us to church each Sunday, my mom offered us spirituality during the week. She was curious about everything. The house was littered with books about the sacred, profane, and paranormal. She reveled in history, scandal, and alternative points of view. She was a devil's advocate who helped balance a house heavy with conservative dogma. We read the Bible on Sunday, but Monday through Saturday, we perused books on psychic pets, the Bermuda triangle, famous hauntings, and conspiracy theories.

4) Scholastic achievement ... or "I expect you to do well." A's meant freedom, B's meant do your homework with the TV and radio off, C's meant you are getting a tutor, and D's meant martial law. My parents felt grades were the canary in the obscure, coal mine existence of an adolescent. There was no tolerance for poor academic performance.

However, there was, at least from my mother, patient recognition that each kid learns differently. When I was a third grader, this belief led to an interesting altercation between my mother and a school counselor who never had a chance.

"He just can't sit still," my mother said. "I think he gets it from my father, whom everyone refers to as 'George Blast-off.' He can't stop moving. If Dad's not working, he's golfing or planting his monster gardens with tomatoes the size of basketballs. Really. It's quite amazing."

"Ma'am, I know this difficult, but have you ever considered Ritalin? I mean, it's a big step, but clinically it's proven to help many hyperactive kids." The voice sounded vacant and bored, like the conductor who mindlessly asked for our ticket on the Amtrak train to San Diego.

"Ritalin? Oh, no, no, no. Really, I don't think so. I'd rather have him twitching like a worm on hot pavement than jumping out a third-story window yelling, 'Look at me, I can fly,' thank you very much. Boys are wiggly creatures. They're always making noises and shifting around to liberate some body part."

As my mother and a baby-faced school psychologist spoke, I was in the next room, swaying like a palm tree on top of a wide oak worktable to see how far I could lean headlong without falling off. I peeked around the corner to spy on my mother and the youthful counselor with the flattop haircut.

"Look, Mrs. Turpin, Michael has a 'D' in citizenship. He's a very friendly boy, but he's disrupting the other students. He talks in class, won't stay in his seat, and today he provoked one of our special education kids into chasing him around the room during rest time. I believe he's suffering from hyperactivity syndrome or possibly some type of undiagnosed personality disorder."

My mother's tone went serial-killer cold. I knew that voice. It was a declaration of war: the seven seconds before the bomb was dropped and life as one knew it would be forever changed.

"Now whom are we talking about, Mister Crimms? It's my understanding that the boy in question is quite enormous—a lot bigger and older than Michael—and it would be unnatural not to run if someone older and larger was pursuing you. That's a sign of intelligence. Exactly how long have you been employed by the district?"

"Now, Ma'am, if you're questioning my experience..."

"Just answer my question, young man."

"Well, if you must know, I finished my graduate degree in pediatric psychology from St. Mary's last year, and I am getting my PhD from USC." He sounded officious and offended. "Look, I have seen methylphenidate work very well on children to help them focus."

"Mr. Crimms, you know, I've done my research, too. A child's hyperactivity can stem from a number of organic sources such as sugar, caffeine, food allergies, and other environmental factors. Why would you want to dope him up without ruling out all other factors first? How do you explain his high marks in all the subject-matter tests? He is intellectually in the top ten percent on all tests."

She composed herself. "With the exception of physical education, my son is a very committed student. He does have an aversion to organized exercise. He hates PE but plays Little League and YMCA football. On any given day, he'll spend hours out of doors."

"Ma'am, some savants have been documented to possess extremely gifted intellects, but they lack social filters and controls. These syndromes stem from innate behaviors and chemical imbalances that medication can help to mute."

"Chemical imbalances? Are you a student psychologist or Nurse Ratched? Have you read *One Flew Over the Cuckoo's Nest*, Mr. Crimms? It seems modern medicine cannot always cure what we have the capacity to remedy ourselves. It's as much about self-esteem as it is about brain chemistry."

She stood up and walked into the foyer clutching my wrist. As she turned to leave the office, she bullwhipped one last barb at the fledgling educator: "What's next? Shock therapy?"

My mother would always get in the last word. In a scene that would repeat itself with each of her sons over many years, she rushed me out of the nurse's office. A moment later, she stopped and looked down at me, smiling.

"Tomorrow, we're weaning you off that damn Mountain Dew and Pop-Tarts!" Her cure worked better than Ritalin would have and as time wore on, further research proved her right in nearly every case.

She insisted on being informed about our lives. She had the inside scoop on every person who made up our uneven world—teachers, friends, coaches, parents of friends. All this from a woman who dropped out of college as a sophomore to marry a penniless army second lieutenant and returned thirty years later to complete her degree.

In the wild '70s, she became a self-anointed DEA officer. She understood that a kid with red eyes and the pungent smell of smoke around him probably had not been out fighting forest fires or struck by lightning. Like a champion contestant on Name That Vice, she could identify bad behavior at a thousand yards and always made sure we knew that she knew. Her candor and caring made it safe for us, and often for our friends, to confess issues she could adroitly handle.

Her passion was the latest technology—and useless gadgetry. While this gave our family a critical start on personal computers well before most house-holds knew that a Mac was anything but a burger, it also resulted in weird experiments: food being preserved under pyramids (Pyramid Power was big in the '70s), dietetic forays—all carbohydrates, no carbohydrates, all fish, no fish, no fat, all rice, all protein, Carnation Instant Breakfast, Space Sticks, and Tang ("If the astronauts can drink it, so can you boys."). Our house was a grand social and technological experiment in a period of great societal change. The twentieth-century matriarch and the seventeenth-century monarch managed the yin and yang of competing opinions, always agreeing on what mattered most.

⚒

Our New Age mother read countless books on dream interpretation, from Freud, Jung, and Cayce to the beliefs of Native American shamans. She ex-plained that she was more a follower of Jung than of Freud. Freud ascribed to people a competing set of mental forces—the subconscious Id and the con-scious Super Ego. The irresistible force of hidden desire (often felt most keenly by teenagers) clashed each night with the immovable objects of temporal re-straint (authority figures, the largest of those being the T-Rex). As the mind worked through these physical and emotional challenges, it painted mental canvases with colors and images more complex and bizarre than any fashioned by Picasso or Chagall.

In my mother's mind, Jung must have been the more experienced parent. He did not seek to interpret dreams as an interconnected tableau of sexual symbols requiring therapeutic intervention but as a collateral universe where the subconscious mind worked furiously over problems, unresolved issues, philosophical conundrums, and latent desires.

As we struggled with our father's religious orthodoxy, we also listened to our mother, who explained that the Bible was filled with examples in which

God chose to appear to individuals in dreams and through these encounters to convey a divine message. The ancient Greeks and Egyptians considered dreams as omens and harbingers of important events. Each society and religion maintained a social order in which those who could decipher the hieroglyphics of dreams—elders, medicine men, oracles, and sages—were raised to positions of prestige and power.

My mother understood that four boys were a breeding ground for germs and adolescent neurosis. She preferred to organically unravel each twitch and tic, helping us understand the demons that occasionally set up shop in our vulnerable minds. Nurture would win out over nature and the subconscious would always point out the bodies that rested at the bottom of a child's mind. The minutes before we fell asleep were the times when we were likely to give up secrets and reveal clues to our strange fear-based behavior.

In the last ten minutes of every night, she would appear like Florence Nightingale, the angel of the nightlight, gently extracting the day's mental splinters of bullies, bad teachers, first crushes, bad choices, and the irrational phantasms that arose out of sibling disinformation.

I always felt that I was her favorite, but in fact I was simply the most neurotic of our four-man cadre. She seemed to spend more time with me than the others, interpreting my behavior and my dreams, reassuring me that one day my twitching cement-pipe legs and monkey-mind attention span would morph into a grown man and athlete.

"Michael, dreams where you are being chased or can't get out away from something are the workings of your subconscious mind trying to solve problems. It's healthy. The reveries where you fly or move things with your mind? Those are power dreams. You may even be in astral flight where your soul is out exploring in the world. I often wonder what you were in a past life. I am sure you were a kind king or perhaps a Shaolin warrior." I smiled, thinking of myself as a benevolent monarch or a flying lethal weapon, perforating a knot of evildoers with a soaring kick and arm chop.

My father, a trim and shadowed spectator in the doorway, would wait for my mother, peering into my room but not buying into her "Age of Aquarius B.S."

"Jesus, Ruth, don't fill his head with that crap. He's got one life and he's gotta stop screwing around to make the most out of it."

My mother continued to look down at me, her smile piercing the darkness. "Your father was a Templar Knight in a past life. He likes to fight for what he believes is right." My father shook his head and once again took the Lord's name in vain. "Well, you may be right, though," he admitted. "I'd like to go over to the Middle East and kick some ass again." He laughed as he walked back into the light of the hallway.

My mother ran slender fingers across my scalp. "Such wonderful hair."

"I got a big head. Somebody called me Pumpkin Head today."

"Honey, everyone in our family has big heads. They're full of brains. Third grade is a tough time. You need to ignore the other kids and learn to sit still and focus on what your teacher says. When you're bored and you want to talk to your neighbor, just take out a piece of paper and write down what you want to say. That way the teacher won't get mad at you for disrupting the class. Understand? Here, I got you this."

Turning on the bedside lamp, she opened a white paper bag and handed me a leather-bound book. I opened it and saw that she had written my name on the first page: Property of Michael Turpin. "You write everything you think and feel in here. Draw pictures or doodle. It's a diary and it's better than any silly old pill from a doctor to help you focus."

Months later, my father discovered what was to be the first of many diaries. Inside were primitive hand-drawn pictures of epic World War II battles, monsters, space ships, and racecars, and in almost every picture, there was a kid with a big head who was the clear protagonist in the illustration. He often used x-ray powers from his mind to vanquish the bad guys.

"Jesus H. Christ," my father said. "A shrink would have a field day with this crap. Why in the hell is this kid drawing Captain Pumpkin Head?"

My mother laughed as she ran her fingers through his haircut that grew like straight grass above his unusually large cranium.

"I don't know where he gets it," she said.

Monsters represented my first collision with life's deep mysteries—forces I could not control but might control me, depending on how I responded to them. Later in life, my childhood preoccupations—dinosaurs, sharks, and imaginary beasts—fell away and were replaced by temporal threats such as terrorists, financial insecurities, and a world that seemed to be always on the cusp of chaos. While I may have grown gray, I have never forgotten those first feelings of irrational adolescent fear when I was forced to confront the creatures and demons that lived in the deep forests of my imagination.

In the 1969 film *The Wolfman*, a bloodthirsty lycanthrope prowled the foggy back roads and villages of the Eastern European countryside. Lon Chaney Jr. played Larry Talbot, an American unfortunate warned by a traveling gypsy that he would be bitten by a werewolf and transform into a carnivorous monster at the next full moon.

The Wolfman scared the dog dirt out of me. Once bitten by a werewolf, I would be doomed to become a creature of the night. The fact that werewolves killed their prey during the full moon yet woke up the next morning refreshed and relaxed meant that *anyone* could be a monster. Since I had a bad habit of sleepwalking, I would often wake up in unfamiliar parts of the house. Had I killed an old woman the night before? Was that hair in my teeth?

Did I know any werewolves? I watched to see who ate the extra hamburger and who seemed to enjoy their steak rare.

Because of my preoccupation with these scary stories, horror movies, and comic books with names such as *The Unexpected* and *Tales from the Crypt*, my imagination had no room for rational thought to filter the ghosts, demonic possessions, and phantasms. My obsessions turned inevitably to irrational fear, and I began to hear noises under my bed and see monsters in scabrous shadows.

The fear became so acute I literally found it impossible to walk the ten feet of hallway from my bedroom to the bathroom. So, like most red-blooded eight-year-olds, I improvised. If awakened during the black hours between midnight and five a.m., I peed behind the bedroom door.

For weeks, my solution worked beautifully until, to my dread, the cat also started to relieve herself in the same spot. At first I whisked her away, but I realized that during school hours she would probably use my room as a litter box.

I decided to kill the increasingly stinging odor of ammonia with a bottle of my father's English Leather cologne. The mixture of cologne and urine created a pungent scent reminiscent of the public restroom at Poncho and Kenny's local barbershop. However, the new bouquet was now potent enough to repulse the cat, who would no longer even enter my bedroom.

"What the hell is that goddamn smell?" my dad asked as he came into my room. I was jolted by the thought that my father might discover my secret. Being a young boy, I was highly skilled at the art of diversion and redirected his attention to my recently organized desk drawer and numerous questions about his job.

He shook his head, still unable to find the epicenter of the miasma. "I swear to God if I catch either that cat or dog upstairs, I am going to tie them to the back of a truck." I thought about implicating the animals, but I loved them too much to risk that he might lash them to a moving van. I went to bed each night declaring that this would be the night I would brave the darkness for the sake of the pets and personal hygiene, but each time I awoke, I could not bear the thought of having my trachea ripped out by Larry Talbot in his Wolfman persona.

Every night, I stared at the Aurora plastic models with the glowing faces and hands I had constructed—The Wolfman, The Creature from the Black Lagoon, and Dracula. I would turn on my radio to listen to the voice of midnight DJs as if to reassure myself that others were awake somewhere. Like clockwork, the song "Nights in White Satin" would moan like a dirge out of the weak il-luminated light of my AM radio. The Moody Blues would croon hauntingly, "Breathe deep, the gathering gloom...." By the time the British voice asked the listener, "and which is an illusion?" I was utterly freaked out and convinced that outside my room the undead waited patiently to eat my face.

By day I was a young, invincible fear junkie wanting to hear every gory detail about every scary thing that ever happened to anyone, particularly to kids my age. My brother was very accommodating, sharing stories of escaped insane asylum inmates with hooks for hands. He told me of ghostly hitchhikers who warned drivers of dangerous roads and people buried alive. By the time he finished a fireside monster story session, I would more likely let my kidneys fail than venture by myself into a darkened toilet.

The day arrived when my mother decided to pull up all the shag rugs to take advantage of the wood floors that rested unappreciated beneath them. In the corner of my bedroom was a rotted hole where the permanently wet wood had yielded to my relentless nightly assaults.

Instead of suspecting me, my mother mistakenly presumed that the shower was leaking. When I arrived home, she was moments away from paying a plumber to tear up the floors to find the leak in the shower tray. In a moment of moral crisis, I confessed that I had been fouling the bedroom corner for eight months. Instead of punishing me, she sat down and laughed until tears poured down her face. "Please just use the toilet," she said. "And stop reading all that garbage that scares you at night." She never did tell my father.

As adolescence accelerated and the obligations of men lay starkly before my brothers and me, she understood we were prone to setbacks and acts of self-sabotage. While my father was ready to cull our family herd of this inferior stock, my mom recognized that boys did not always express themselves clearly and our thoughtless acts were periodic cries for help. On one occasion, my setback became a life-changing lodestar for her as she responded to external threats and helped resolve a nightmare before it became permanent.

It was Career Day at San Marino High School in sunny 1977 Southern California. Our school district was determined to illuminate the intricate machinery of the working world in hopes of aligning students' nascent interests with future vocations.

In homeroom, we were asked to fill out a questionnaire designed to ascertain our strengths, weaknesses, passions, and peccadilloes. The teachers and counselors were told to take this process very seriously, and I recall being reprimanded during the assessment as I rolled my eyes at the questions, which included:

1. Which word best describes you?
    a) Follower
    b) Leader

2. Your best work environment involves:
    a) Working indoors standing up
    b) Working indoors sitting down
    c) Working outdoors standing up
    d) Working outdoors sitting down.

I looked for the missing answer: e) none of the above. A lot depended on if I had to sweat or walk very far to work. Did the job pay at least four dollars an hour? Could I perform this task while watching TV? Would someone need to inspect my work before I could go home for the night?

I needed to clarify these questions. I raised my hand. "I don't know, Turpin," whispered my perpetually annoyed homeroom teacher. "Just try to find one that describes you."

"What if none of them describes me?" I chirped.

"Don't get smart, mister," he scolded. "You have fifteen more minutes."

The test results were collected, tabulated, and cross-referenced with our most recent grades. Together these data were somehow triangulated to provide a rich social X-ray into our potential as contributing members of society. Once we were labeled and categorized, we were scheduled to meet with our "counselors" to discuss the findings.

My mother was highly skeptical of the educational gimmicks that periodically worked their way through our school district. Guiding four sons from elementary through high school, she had experienced every type of charlatan and their educational reforms. She had seen them all: the academics, the socialists, and the 26-year-old Ivy League PhDs as they cycled through the school district as teachers, principals, and superintendents. She distrusted profiling tests that attempted to pigeonhole children early in their development, especially during the sophomore year, when most kids were still trying to understand rudimentary geometry and the deep mysteries of the opposite sex.

The morning of my career day debrief, I received a packet that explained the profile testing methodology. I was excited. Perhaps the results would be my personal burning bush, revealing to me my predisposition to be an entertainment czar or an international import/export mogul. I went into my counselor's office where he sat, feet on his desk and nursing a mug of coffee with the word "Coach" stenciled on its side. "Well, Turpin, let's see what we have here."

He opened an official-looking testing scorecard that was pre-populated with graphs, charts, and complicated percentages. He looked at it as if it were written in Aramaic. He clearly had no clue what the bar charts and median scores meant. I held my breath. "So, it says here, let's see, that you...should really consider a career as a fish and game warden."

I waited for more, but that was it. "You know, Coach, my dad's in advertising. Does it say anything about that? I'm also a pretty good artist and I actually like English." He seemed stumped that I had not just accepted my fate. He hesitated and handed me a brochure titled "Fish and Game Warden: A life of adventure." Everyone had been talking all day about careers. The girl behind me was going to be in international fashion. The straight-A math savant in the front row of my geometry class was going to be a banker. And moi? I was going to arrest people for illegal fires and not carrying a fishing license.

I didn't say anything at dinner that night, but I was worried. I had been programmed by my father to believe that any vocation involving a shovel, heavy machinery, or a shirt with my name stenciled on it was a vine that would bear limited fruit. Success did not come from sitting in a fire tower glancing across an ocean of evergreens looking for a puff of smoke.

I did not tell my mother, but as usual she discovered the truth. She had recovered the crumpled fish and game warden brochure in my blue jeans pocket. She confronted me, and I promptly spilled my troubled guts. She listened intently but was secretly seething. She was also concerned that Coach was slated to be my college counselor.

It was at this moment that she privately declared war on the school district and their college admissions counseling program. To protect her boys and their friends, she would go into business for herself as a college applications consultant. In retrospect, it was a brilliant move for a woman who had subordinated much of her own life to keeping four potential felons on the straight path toward college. Her competitors were part-time educators and overworked, multitasking idealists. Marketing would not be a problem. She was already somewhat of a micro-celebrity among other women in our town for her candor and pragmatism in dealing with boys.

Over the next ten years, she took on hundreds of surrogate children and their parents as clients. She learned every loophole, admissions officer preference, essay style, and mood of universities across the country. She also could divine those oh-so-important intangibles within the first hour of meeting a kid: Was the student an overachiever or underachiever? Was he/she spending too much time smoking dope in the east parking lot? Did the kid have undetected learning disabilities? She could tell who was mature enough to handle a larger university and which student would likely never be heard from again if he entered some massive state school.

She was tough and candid with her protégés but universally admired by kids and parents alike. There was only one casualty: my father, who could not understand her need to work and fill his home with teenagers after he had struggled so hard to get them out. He kept urging her to sell her business or quit. Her hours were killing him, as she was often unavailable to cook his dinner or talk with him when he staggered in from a business trip. He tried to put his foot down. She ignored him.

The worm turned one spring when my father decided to join an exclusive business club and found that the chairman of the selection committee was not as familiar with him as he was with his wife.

"Hmm. Turpin. Your wife isn't Ruth Turpin, is she?"

"Yes, she is."

"Hell!" the gruff chairman broke into a Cheshire cat grin. "This man's wife helped get my daughter into Stanford. The least I can do is let her husband into the club."

That night he arrived home and recounted the story to my mom. I think he finally understood that helping all these kids was her sweet revenge on the school district as well as her personal antidote to the emotional trauma of an empty nest. To this day, a year does not go by that someone will not approach me or one of my now-successful siblings with a quizzical look and say, "Is your mom Ruth Turpin?"

Yes, she is. Boy Whisperer. She-Rex. Protector of Teens and Secrets. Mater ex Machina.

I Sing the Body Eccentric

Two Abs, Hold the Sauce

*"In a man's middle years there is scarcely a part of the body
he would hesitate to turn over to the proper authorities."*
—E.B. WHITE

MIDDLE AGE CREEPS up on you like a mugger. It starts when friends come over, point to your wedding picture, and say, "Is that *you*?"

"No, it's not me," I laugh sarcastically. "This is Caroline's second marriage. That tan, svelte pool boy you see with her in the snapshot was her first husband. He died in a mysterious accident at a Dunkin' Donuts." I lean in. "We don't talk about him anymore. Now she has a fetish for fiftyish men who appear to be in their second trimester."

"Oh, he's just being silly," she interjects. She's always indirectly apologizing for my obtuse cynicism.

Physical transformation is subtle and insidious. You lose a loop in the belt. The collar tightens. You appreciate elastic. It's nature's way of slowly introducing you to mortality. It starts the way wet, heavy snow gently glides off a pine branch after a storm. The snow hits the ground, rolls innocently downhill, and eventually ends up as an avalanche.

My avalanche began with faint warning signs. Years of daily running, pickup basketball, weight lifting, work, children, and apathy began to take their toll. The tailor who kept letting out my slacks finally told me in broken English that there was "no more anything to work with." I had used up all the fabric there was.

Determined to hold off gravity, I stubbornly insisted on wearing pants two sizes too small. I recall one morning when I squeezed into my pinstripe power suit for a very important meeting. I said goodbye to my family as if I were holding my breath the way the kids do when they pass a cemetery.

Arriving at the client presentation, I found that the meeting already had begun. When I sat down—a little too quickly—I heard a sudden, loud ping as a flying object struck a water glass and the client put a hand to her cheek as if to check for blood. The person seated next to her bent over with a perplexed look and then rose, smiling and holding up a button—the very button that had shot off my pants like an assassin's bullet. "Anyone want to claim this?" he said.

Weeks later, I was traveling to Atlanta to give a speech when I suffered another indignity. As I leaned down to pick up my briefcase after hailing a taxi at Hartsfield airport, I heard a pronounced rip and felt cool air swirling around my BVDs. Still in denial, I gingerly felt the top of the tear and turned to the cab driver. "Is it bad?" I asked. He laughed and through toothless, heaving guffaws drawled, "Man, you coul' drahve a truck through that hole."

My hellish day was just beginning, as it was 7:45 a.m. and in only forty-five minutes, I was speaking to three hundred people. We drove to the hotel in Buckhead as I looked for any kind of clothing store. Finally spying an Old Navy outlet, I darted up to the door only to discover they didn't open until nine o'clock.

Wait, there was movement inside! Teenaged girls were folding merchandise and checking displays. I pounded on the window, turned around, and showed them my ripped pants. They looked shocked as they yelled at the apparent flasher, "Please, mistah, jus' go 'way." Ten minutes later two police patrol cars arrived (things must have been slow in Buckhead that day). The older officer was quite sympathetic as he considered my underwear, while his younger partner had a difficult time suffocating his laughter. Finally a manager over the age of 21 appeared, correctly assessed my situation, and let me in.

I arrived at my speaking engagement a half-hour late and began my presentation with an apology. "There is a problem with healthcare in America and I am part of it." I then held up the pants ripped from back to crotch. Laughter washed over me.

It is true I am prone to excess. This trait is magnified by being married to someone who, after three children, weighs within two pounds of what she did the day we were married. She stops eating when she is full. She leaves half her dessert on her plate. She eats more slowly than a septuagenarian with a mouth of loose dentures. Moderation is her mantra. She is an alien.

My mantra, however, was "More is better." I continued to find ways of rationalizing my weight gain. I avoided mirrors before or after a shower. I struck a particular pose as I dressed each morning. The light caught me in such a way that I could believe the apple fritter I had devoured the day before had had no real impact. I was firmly now in the land of the fat-guy suits—the ones you keep in your closet just in case you put on an extra ten pounds, or more.

I prayed that pleats would not go out of style. Thank God for pleats. Pleats are a big man's best friend. Pleats soothe you: "You know what? If God wanted you skinny, your best friend would be a gastric bypass surgeon." They tease you: "So what if your butt is so big it looks like you are being followed." Or they berate you: "You're so fat, you could have three wives and they probably would never meet." I shrugged it off. I'm just big-boned, I thought, and my blood sugar is a little more spirited than the next guy's.

It finally came to a head after a vacation to the Bahamas and the pictures were returned from CVS. I could not believe how large I had become. With a little eye black and white paint, I could have been cast as the orca's younger brother in *Free Willy*. It was time to head into a gym. Just one last cinnamon roll...

I walked into the local fitness club and turned myself over to Steve and Jamal, trainers who, after one week, I believed to be escaped war criminals from some distant land. Who else would delight in the inhuman sounds that escaped my body as they subjected me to burpees, box-jumps and flipping a 230-pound tractor-trailer tire? Yet their counsel, weights, cardio, and fitness regimen have done wonders for me, and the nagging little irritations—sleeplessness, heartburn, and midday munchies—that plagued me for years began their retreat, replaced by a surge of energy and confidence. I was shocked one day, when I took off my shirt and saw an abdominal muscle. I had a two-pack!

I prefer smaller gyms because there are fewer witnesses. I don't delude myself into thinking anyone under the age of 40 even notices me. Yet it is my salvation, a place where I can sweat away the demons of excess in relative anonymity. That is not to say I no longer hear the siren's call of M&Ms or cookie dough. However, the fitness routine has given me the balance I lacked for so many years and made it less likely I will ever need to appear as the fattest guy on *The Biggest Loser*. My fat pants now feel too big and I am making progress into the medium and skinny sections of my closet.

Whenever I get the temptation to slide back into fritters and fried foods, I reach down and feel around for that upper abdominal. Wait, wait. Ah, there it is.

53 Is the New 38

*"Middle Age is where your broad mind and your
narrow waist begin to change places."*
—JOHN CROSSMAN

I NEVER TOOK a regular medication for an ongoing condition before I was in my forties. My mother did not believe in pills. She was one part Christian Scientist and two parts Inuit who subscribed to the notion that sick children, like old people, should be set outside the igloo at night and if they were still alive in the morning, they could be allowed to rejoin the family. Illness and chronic conditions plagued people like old man Norton, who lived across the street. At 85, he suffered from heart failure and diabetes, and it seemed like every other week they were lopping off one of his appendages as a sort of burnt offering to his disease. It was a preview of a movie I hoped never to see.

When we were kids, we averted our eyes from the vagaries of aging, not so much out of denial but out of some misguided sense that old age only happened to other people. Deep down, we knew it would be waiting for us, like that German shepherd that sometimes chased us on our bikes.

On sunny afternoons, I occasionally glimpsed Mr. Norton and he would wave to me from his wheel chair—all two arms, one foot and a half-leg. It freaked me out and I made a pact with myself that I would never succumb to old age. I would cheat it and commit to a life either so reckless or physically vigorous that chronic disease would simply shrug and pass me by. I would go out in a flash, perhaps spontaneously combusting on a rock-and-roll stage or slowly asphyxiating on the side of Mount Everest after rescuing a dozen Sherpas trapped inside a crevasse on the Khumbu Icefall.

Despite my best efforts to remain a juvenile, middle age finally collared me. I am now bemused by my own denial—a self-deception that seeps in like lugubrious fog and obscures moments of self-reflection. I seek friendships with people who conserve electricity; their energy-saver bulbs have a sort of muted Blanche Dubois quality that fails to expose my true age. I prefer spandex, "comfortable" Levis, and larger versions of everything. I wear my shirt outside my pants and avoid stripes, which turn me into a large Fabergé egg. My wedding day 33-inch waist has eroded like a Florida sinkhole, widening to 38 inches, a metric that should only define the circumference of old trees and an athlete's vertical leap at a football combine. A protective shell has formed near the top of my solar plexus. It feels like a muscle but I am being told it is fat—presumably being stored in the event the Food Emporium ever goes on strike.

Global warming has begun. The canard that only women have hot flashes could not be less accurate. When we are large and in charge, we feel warm all the time. In a single winter day, I am both sweating and freezing as I move from windy, frigid streets to offices hotter than a sweat lodge. In summer, I advocate the notion that thermometers should be calibrated by weight, not by temperature, as I would prefer to set the air conditioner to a cool 235 pounds each night instead of the balmy 105 pounds favored by my wife.

Some of us start driving sports cars because they remind us of a time when we could sit comfortably in the middle seat of an airplane without feeling like a human s'more. People whisper when they see the new ride: "Tsk, tsk. He's having a mid-life crisis." Well, folks, I'm here to tell you that in 1986, when I did look good enough to drive a convertible, I did not have two dimes to rub together and drove a puke-green Renault Alliance, which not unlike the French who built it, would routinely sit down in the middle of a job and go on strike. We sports car drivers are not compensating for anything. We're just enjoying the fruits of our hard labor and perhaps hoping not to be as invisible as we feel.

At 53, the body started paying me back. The knees went first. Years of sports and running, coupled with a pathetic version of stretching that involved making one effort to briefly touch my toes, gave me a bulging disc and hamstrings as tight as a cat-gut mandolin. The shoulders followed. Years of poor technique in the weight room, a mediocre baseball career, and annual trips to the emergency room after countless injuries in my family's Turkey Bowl football games rewarded me with clicking joints reminiscent of a playing card hitting the spokes of a bicycle tire.

The latest manifestation of mortal decline occurred at Halloween while I was sucking on one of the many Tootsie Pops I appropriated from my youngest son, informing him that he must pay "a toll to the troll." He might as well get used to being taxed now.

As I succumbed to the inevitable urge to bite the hard candy, my right molar broke off like an Antarctic ice shelf. It turned out to be an eleven-hundred-dollar piece of candy and my first crown. Thinking back, I'm sure old man Norton had his fair share of crowns, but I had always assumed my teeth would be indestructible—at least I thought so in college when I opened beer bottles with them.

Middle age now means moderation, which is a dirty word. The whole diet thing is a touchy subject in any marriage marked by a weight imbalance. Yet my wife tolerates me and often travels great verbal distances to find just the right word for self-improvement. I listen in amusement, wondering how my spouse segues from ISIS to my losing ten pounds. It's diplomatic genius. She ought to work at the UN. She uses code words to hint at lack of restraint—patronizing placeholders such as "healthy," "balanced," and my favorite: "portion control."

I'm grateful the dog does not seem perturbed by my slow disintegration. He moves at my speed, an adoring shadow that has fallen in love with my insides and considers my outsides merely an extra coat of fur. The dog and I agree on the true definition of portion control: eat until you're going to be sick. Normally, when he overeats, he goes outside, munches on some grass, returns, and throws it all up on a nice rug. I just lie down and moan, informing my wife that I think I have the stomach flu. Meanwhile, my son comes into the room to ask who ate all the cupcakes. I try to blame the dog but he is in the other room throwing up grass.

I am suddenly noticing that everything in the fridge is now low fat. I search for sweets at midnight and the cupboards are filled with healthy things: nuts, dates, and dried apricots. This is no longer my house; it's a spice market in Baghdad. I search my spouse's favorite hiding places including the cleverest default: the microwave. I am mildly insulted at our passive-aggressive war of weight and wits, but hey, game on. She is Holmes and I am her archenemy Professor More For Me. The dinners are very healthy with portions smaller than those in a French restaurant. Like Oliver Twist, I keep waiting for seconds, but she has cleverly prepared only enough for one serving. "More? You want... more?"

It's not that I don't try. However, the majority of calories I consume occur between seven p.m. and midnight. Night eating is a problem, and the result eventually hits every man. The night arrives when you go to bed on a full stomach and wake up coughing with the sensation of napalm in your throat. My first thought was I was turning into a dragon and that perhaps I just needed to light a match to give birth to the fire in my esophagus. The next thing I knew I was exchanging Zantac and Nexium with my golf buddies like a couple of crackheads in an alleyway.

Family photos also become an issue. It's always subtle. One of the kids or my wife will say, "Here's a good one of you," with profound encouragement. This is code for, "You look like the Hindenburg or a human manatee in most of these shots, but this photo (where we can't see your face), may meet your denial criteria."

I now find myself fighting over Christmas photos more than the kids: "Oh, great, we don't need to tell them where this was taken because from this angle, I look like Asia Minor." In the end, we decide to feature only the kids, and I finally concede to one couples photo that will be on the inside of the card.

I can almost hear the Christmas card comments, "Wow, she looks great!" Pause. "And he looks...um...prosperous!" The absence of praise should be construed as criticism. Yes, 53 has become the new 38. Thirty-eights are everywhere: 38-inch waists, a maximum of 38 push-ups, 38 minutes of jogging before the knee feels as if it's been swatted by Malaysian riot police, and 38 ways to hear someone say, "I wouldn't wear that if I were you."

Life has turned quickly from "dos" to "don'ts." The new regulations: Don't eat fatty foods. Don't eat meat. Don't eat refined sugar. Don't eat gluten. ("I'd actually like an extra helping of gluten, please, waitress, and can you fry it into a little fritter so I can drizzle honey on it?")

At 53, my superhero outfit is a little tight, but it's my job to be a "roll" model for other middle-aged manatees. You want us on that wall. You need us on that wall. We just can't all climb up on it at the same time or it might shatter. We have our purpose. We make the skinny people feel good, and we aren't afraid to be the "before" picture in some ad touting self-improvement.

We may be middle-aged, but inside our 53 is a 38 and underneath that it is a 33. You know, sort of like a burrito. I remember burritos.

A Touch of Grey

"There is only one cure for grey hair. It was invented by a Frenchman. It is called the guillotine."
—P.G. WODEHOUSE

THE FIRST GREY hair showed up when I was seventeen. The sudden loss of melanin in this particular follicle coincidentally followed my first Grateful Dead concert. It seemed a novelty at the time: a rare phenomenon like corn snow that occasionally fell for two minutes every few years in Los Angeles and then melted quickly against the wet, warm asphalt. That single hair, however, was the harbinger of a silver flood that would transform me from ingénue to elder statesman by the age of thirty.

Dickens once said, "Regrets are the natural property of grey hairs." While scientists insist the process of greying is genetic, I am convinced that I earned most of my silver the hard way. I am a firm believer that each grey hair is a reward for life's travails: telling your boss what you really think; hitting a seventeen at the blackjack table with your semester's spending money on the line; losing your toddler in a department store for an hour only to have her emerge laughing from a circular clothes rack where she had watched you search as you muttered, "She's going to kill me. She's going to kill me!" It's having your computer-literate child hack through every parental control application you have installed. It is the call at 3 a.m.

Some people run from the grey. They use cosmetic products to mask it. A guy I know is quite a bit past fifty, but he has hair blacker than a bowling ball at Rip Van Winkle Lanes. It's not good genetics. It's bad shoe polish. Another acquaintance nurtures a single strand of hair that could stretch across the state of Utah. Each morning he lovingly winds that massive black mamba around his head, carefully avoiding swim parties, wind tunnels, and head massages.

Grey is a state of mind. Youthful Satchel Paige, the oldest major leaguer of his day, debuted for the Cleveland Indians at age 42 after years as a star in the Negro Leagues. He was the first African-American player in the American League. Paige was constantly asked about his age. He retorted, "If you did not know how old you are, how old would you be?"

For me, it's only as a result of mirrors and cameras that I am reminded that I have physically yielded to middle age. I still feel 20 years old and my spouse will attest that I maintain a highly childish, warped sense of humor and see comedy everywhere, from growing up in a house full of boys to Will Ferrell to neo-conservatives to movies such as *This is Spinal Tap* and *The Big Lebowski* to, well, everything.

Certainly my inability to be serious for sustained periods of time has sometimes proved a social impediment. However, immaturity occasionally serves as a tender bridge to a surly teenager or a disgruntled friend. It is also healthy. It's a known fact that one's immune system is reinforced through the simple act of laughter. Laughing suppresses the release of cortisol and epinephrine, two chemicals known to attack the immune system. Studies show that laughter activates T and B cells and a variety of others that fight viruses, among other benefits.

A healthy response to life begins with learning to laugh at oneself. Grey hair gives you permission. It's a rite of passage and a merit badge that suggests you have been around long enough to know that Mel Tormé was not a forward for the New York Knicks, Hunter S. Thompson was not the thirty-ninth President, and Jerry Garcia is not an ice cream.

A silver streak means you may have felt the deep ache of losing a close friend to illness. It means you have known disappointment. Grey signals that you are on your way to realizing the only person who can make you happy is you. It means you understand that comedy is tragedy plus time, and that you never burn a bridge because you invariably need to cross it again. Grey hair teaches you to be careful how you treat people on the way up because you will meet them again on the way down. A little frost around the temples means you understand that expectations can become resentments.

A sprinkling of grey means you probably have lost something you could not afford to lose. You most likely have discovered that you can't control life but you can control how you react to it. Some salt and pepper accompanies your finally figuring out that the more you focus on other people, the less likely you are to feel sorry for yourself. You understand that fame and fortune can be a trap and that your legacy will be how many lives you have touched, not what you have accumulated. You understand that class is style, not stature.

Let's face it, our society celebrates youth and has a tendency to view grey the way some Americans view Europe—old, past its prime, and seemingly jealous of the adolescent that has arrived to assume the role of the alpha. Youth may have size, strength, and a sense of immortality but lacks the perspective that comes with age and vicissitudes. Insight is gained through pain and the bitter experience of getting what you think you want only to find it is not what you needed. Grey is humility. It is being able to say "I'm sorry," but not spend the rest of your life self-flagellating. It is being able to laugh at your own expense, not at someone else's. Grey may lack the visceral allure of youth but it radiates the intrinsic beauty of a centered soul. In the end, age teaches us that nothing in the world is black and white.

Everything, as the Grateful Dead suggest, has a "touch of grey."

Ask Jack

*"Fashion is a form of ugliness so intolerable that
we have to alter it every six months."*
—OSCAR WILDE

I T WAS A cloudless September Saturday full of Indian summer promises. I had emerged from my closet ready to pace the sidelines of two football fields. I had on my usual ensemble—white cargo pants, black tee shirt, flip-flops, backward-facing baseball cap, and retro Ray-Bans.

"Oh, oh, oh," I heard. At first I thought my partner was talking to the dog. It was that same lilting expression she utters when chastising a pet for coveting the food on the counter. "Are you going to wear that today?" came from the opposite closet. "It's after Labor Day. Time to put away the white shorts."

This was not the first time I had been rounded up by the fashion police. During twenty-some years of marriage, I have been picked up more times than a Hollywood Boulevard streetwalker. I was feeling defensive knowing that in more than a half-century I had made little progress against my style disability.

"Who made that rule up anyway?" I retorted. I believe it was canny group of mothers sick of scrubbing summer-stained white garments, although my mother always appreciated white as a road map to what we had eaten and where we had been during the previous twelve hours.

I asked around town. People shrugged. "It's just the way we've always done things." It seemed everyone in the East had been living by this ancient code. Growing up in California, however, I abided by no Labor Day rule. California fashion comprised three styles: surfer, casual, and preppy.

As the third of four boys, I was a fashion orphan condemned to battered hand-me-downs that were always out of style. I was not allowed to have an opinion about clothes, so my fashion sense was stunted from an early age. To complicate things, I was cursed with the physique of a squat Irish peat-bog worker, while my older brothers were blessed with continental European metabolisms and the builds of clothing store mannequins. I was meant to wear an animal skin, not lightweight cotton chinos.

My eldest brother, Miles, was elegant and slender, resembling a youthful Cary Grant. He possessed instinctive élan and style and actually enjoyed clothes shopping with my mother. He did not get his apparel at any old department store. No, he purchased his wardrobe at a men's store called Atkinson's.

Atkinson's was very posh. The attractive girl behind the counter that no public school boy would never get to date because she went to a private, all-girls high school placed our purchases in bright red boxes, sealing them with canary-yellow ribbons. The salesmen were a natty, sartorial flock of 30-something ex-USC frat boys who would coo and fawn over my elegant sibling. They would then turn their disappointed gazes on me, saying to my mother, "I am not sure we have anything in *his* size."

It was at that point that I rejected the superficial uniform of the preppies and the posers. I would dress like a jock. For more formal occasions with young women, I would perhaps turn my baseball cap to the front.

I secretly envied those tailored Trojans and wanted to be like them, but I could never pull off the latest look. I seemed to have a bent antenna when it came to understanding that madras shorts and a striped button-down shirt don't go together unless you are trying to find out which of your friends has epilepsy.

As I got older, I picked up a few sound bites that only distorted my narrow understanding of fashion. "If you have a larger physique, you should wear black. It is a slimming color." I was all for slimming and proceeded to dress like the Viet Cong until someone asked me if I was Johnny Cash's brother. When someone else suggested that all black meant I vacationed with Satan, ate bats' heads, and listened to Ozzie Osbourne, I abandoned my monochromatic scheme. If I was, as my mother suggested, what I wore, then I was a Crayola box with only two colors.

It got worse when I left the cocoon of my Southern California suburb for college. I recall going to parties with East Coast guys who wore their polo shirts with the collars up, jetty red shorts, and cordovan penny loafers. This bizarre uniform made them look like emasculated, metrosexual vampires. Nonetheless, they looked at me as if I had just gotten off work from my construction job, and the girls seemed to naturally gravitate toward the *sofisticatezza* of these peculiar specimens.

Marriage brought me a spouse determined to sandpaper my rough edges. However, I was often caught attempting to leave the house in clothes that were out of season, too short, too long, stained, torn, garish, brutish, or just plain pathetic. I started receiving clothing as gifts.

That's when I knew I was officially an adult; I got clothes for Christmas and birthdays. They were not clothes I would pick out. They were the clothes purchased by someone trying to turn me into an accidental fashionisto. Dark shirts with weird flaring collars, jeans with meticulously fake faded spots, and funky euro shoes with long, elfin tips. If I actually wore all of these clothes, I surely would not be able to walk five feet.

I had to take back control of my wardrobe, but I knew I could not make it alone. I needed a wingman. And one day while roaming the Web, I stumbled upon Jack: J. Crew's Men's Stylist. I bored deeper into cyberspace and found a treasure trove of trend-setting websites, all promising to cure me of my lifelong fashion myopia. There was now a safe place for the legions of garment geeks to ask embarrassing questions such as, "What can I wear to a beach wedding?" "What are the do's and don'ts of sandals?" "How do you dress for winter without looking like a tool?"

Can I wear a tank top to the gym? AskMen.com replied, "*If you must show off the guns, please wear a sleeveless shirt. A-shirts—tank tops associated with* domestic abuse—are not really recommended anywhere (except the bleacher section of a Yankee game)."

What about those guys wearing spandex? "For women, spandex is a privilege, not a right. For men, it is neither. It is a very, very bad mistake."

The websites challenged me and probed. Did I want to be a Trend Setter, Preppy, Hipster, Rocker, Classic, or Sporty Chic? Actually, I just wanted to know whether it was okay to wear my cargo shorts into October. Ask Jack hesitated and then answered, "White or wheat denim long pants work year-round."

Huh?

Screw it, it's eighty degrees and I'm wearin' the white shorts.

Ear Today, Ghoul Tomorrow?

"I don't plan to grow old gracefully. I plan to have face-lifts until my ears meet."
—Rita Rudner

LIFE, FOR MOST mortals, is a zero-sum game. As we enter middle age, we begin receiving past due notices requesting payment for every act of vanity, gluttony, sloth, and stupidity.

As a child growing up on the beaches of Southern California, I endured a perpetual cycle of burn and tan, always followed by a reptilian peeling. In the days when dermatologists existed to treat teens for acne and ancient beachcombers for melanoma, parents did not force kids to lather up with SPF 50 sunscreen. When overexposure to the sun produced second-degree burns, our mothers would simply apply a greasy, white industrial ointment known as zinc oxide to the afflicted area and hustle us back out into the sun.

Like the Aztecs of ancient Mexico, we were a society of sun worshippers. A tan was considered a healthy measure of a man's cultural, physical, and financial prowess. Film stars such as George Hamilton and Robert Wagner personified the benefits of melanin and masculinity. Despite my light eyes and County Kerry skin, I was constantly in search of the savage tan—and the Fates later reminded me of my deal with the devil.

At the ripe young age of thirty-five, I noticed a small patch of flaking skin that never seemed to heal just above my left eye. It was no larger than a thimble top and had a predictable six- to-eight-week sequence of itching, peeling, and healing. I mentioned it in passing to my physician during a rare physical. As a precaution, he sent me to a dermatologist who, after conducting a biopsy, surprised me with a diagnosis of basal cell carcinoma.

My skin doctor further unnerved me by sharing that removal of this negligible blemish would require the assistance of a plastic surgeon, as the site in question had little skin to suture the quarter-sized area that had to be excised. He went on to describe a Frankenstein type of procedure that would graft skin from my temple by twisting it clockwise over the open eyebrow.

I was unnerved by the notion of plastic surgery. I assumed that the only people in need of it were criminals attempting to alter their physical appearances, aging celebrities, and of course, Nancy Pelosi. I instantly recalled the Frank Capra Halloween classic *Arsenic and Old Lace*, in which a sociopathic murderer, played by creepy Raymond Massey, returns home to threaten his family after being disfigured by his drunken plastic surgeon, Peter Lorre. My active imagination transferred his scars to my face—a face not even my dog could love.

I endured the surgery but developed an embarrassing postoperative complication that involved excessive scar tissue accumulating underneath the incision. I appeared to be growing a small horn from my forehead. Because it had been several centuries since horned, pan-flute-playing fauns were in vogue, I was eager to receive a hornectomy. An infection required that I wait six months for this critical second round of plastic surgery. In the interim, I gained a lifetime of insights about my own vanity.

The horn incident left me with a strong motivation to return to my dermatologist every six months to be probed for suspicious moles, foreign freckles, and dubious discolorations. If the doctor found anything, he would deploy his trusty canister of liquid nitrogen and freezer burn the cells gone wild. Aesthetically, my doctor never seemed to consider the fact that I had a social life and that freezer burns across my nose, cheeks, and forehead made me look like someone in the early stages of leprosy. It was inconvenient, but I finally realized that the person who most noticed my burn marks was I.

Fast forward. It had been years since I'd been diagnosed with any epidermal irregularities. I was beginning to think I had finally gotten the skin cancer monkey off my back when the doctor found a small patch of flaking skin on the inside of my ear. What was thought to be a bit of eczema was instead an aggressive squamous cell carcinoma cancer that needed to be removed immediately.

Excision surgery of this sort—called Mohs—involves removing the lesion and any surrounding tissue that might be corrupted by the cancerous cells. The doctor expands the radius of the excision until the adjacent skin is cancer-free. What might start as a laser-thin surgical bore can grow into the Grand Canyon. While preferable to the more medieval types of skin surgeries, which usually resulted in pieces of one's body being removed, Mohs is still an invasive procedure, in this case in an area predominantly comprising cartilage, which is slow to heal, quick to infect, and impossible to disguise. I worried I would look like Van Gogh without the compensating artistic talent.

After a seemingly uneventful surgery, my ear was wrapped and I was sent home to convalesce. The bandage looked like a battlefield medic dressing. It was enormous and came to an unattractive point at the top of my ear. I appeared to be either preparing for a journey to Modor or readying myself for a Star Trek convention.

My spouse did what all good spouses do: she lied to me saying, "You can hardly notice it." She was so confident of its total invisibility she suggested we go to the local varsity football game to get my mind off my disfigurement. I was reluctant to appear in public, as I knew two-thirds of our entire community would be gathered to socialize and stare at my ear. I could envision four-year-old kids scribbling lists they would ask me to give to Santa.

At the football game, I skulked in the shadows like Boo Radley. I lasted two quarters and declared it was time to leave. Later that evening, under a bright vanity mirror light, I surveyed the bullet hole wound and the exposed cartilage. I felt like "Massive Head Wound Harry," a disgusting character made famous by Dana Carvey on *Saturday Night Live*. I second-guessed whether I should have asked the doctor for an appointment with a plastic surgeon.

As a healthcare executive, I had philosophical reservations about elective plastic surgery. Americans spend up to thirteen billion dollars a year on non-essential procedures. What was once a medical profession designed to improve the quality of life for those unfairly dealt deuces in the game of life had become a multibillion-dollar industry catering to the insecurities of a society that glorified youth and whispered promises that physical perfection led to personal happiness. The appearance of youth suggested that you might dodge the hangman's noose and become a modern-day Methuselah.

Despite a regimen of rigorous exercise, certain parts of my body categorically refuse to recognize me as their sovereign. These untamed regions resist my periodic offensives to domesticate them. As I survey my wobbly inner thighs or stubborn love handles, the voice of popular culture chips away at my self-confidence. I could easily see myself getting caught up in the body-image spiral. Fixing one wrinkle could potentially create a cat's cradle of problems. I might become addicted to surgery and within a few years end up looking like a fifteenth-century samurai—or Kenny Rogers. Old Kenny has been stretched more times than salt-water taffy and looks as if he is permanently walking into his own surprise party.

I do not know what it is about middle-aged men and denial. While guys generally age gracefully, they cannot always see the dignity in a salt-and-pepper patina. Take for instance, my hero, Olympic decathlete Bruce Jenner, who, after too many surgeries, resembled the illegitimate offspring of an orange orangutan and an iguana. Bruce, who should have starred in a TV special, *When Good Facelifts Go Bad*, presided for years like a eunuch over a harem of Kardashian/Jenner women. He has now decided to become one of them, and Caitlyn looks much younger than Bruce.

Watching all this desperate vanity made me suddenly self-conscious that I was aging too gracefully. Yet, when my elfin ear finally healed, I stopped worrying that I would forever remind my friends of the Tyson/Holyfield fight. The bandage came off revealing a delicate and noble scar. It might detract from my physical appearance, but in the end, it is another story to be added to my mortal passage. I have come to regard it as one more unique brush stroke on my canvas: a flawed Dorian Gray portrait replete with silver hair, crow's feet, and laugh lines. For now, I will play the cards God gave me, and continue to wage conventional warfare against those physical regions that seem immune to my best intentions. If those vexatious basal cells return and the dermatologist's scalpel reappears, perhaps I'll resign myself to joining a community theatre group and seek to be cast as the malevolent Jonathan Brewster in this year's version of *Arsenic and Old Lace.*

On the Other Side
of the Divide

Postcards Hung on a Distant Mirror

"Most people don't grow up. Most people age. They find parking spaces, honor their credit cards, get married, have children, and call that maturity. What that is, is aging."
—MAYA ANGELOU

O N THE CORNER of my rural street stands an ancient oak that is always first to turn its back on summer. The colors appear unobtrusively, frosting the highest branches and whispering that change has found me once again. Life in a small New England town has its own predictable rhythm of seasons and stages. The dog days of August have been reduced to a collage of digital pictures littered across Facebook pages—a happy memorial to moments when our family once again found each other for adventures across lakes, mountains, and two American coastlines.

My priorities are shifting with middle age as I become keenly aware of the passage of time. A helicopter Boomer, I have spent two decades along a thousand green-grass sidelines and silhouetted in the deep recesses of school auditoriums. I did not want to miss a single moment of my captive constituents' lives. It is in sharp contrast to my own childhood when we were tossed into the wider world as soon as we could master a Schwinn bicycle. Fathers were only seen after 9 p.m. and on weekends.

My dad chuckles at the myriad photographs of our teenagers logging more frequent-flyer miles than a traveling salesman. He wonders whether my insistence on work-life balance is an improvement on his T-Rex parenting or more likely a sign of the permanent blurring of the lines between parent and child and, as such, the decline of Western civilization.

"You don't see the Chinese attending every school concert," he says. It's always about the Chinese.

"Well, Dad, I don't know. I'm not living there. And besides, most Chinese families have only one child."

"I was not supposed to be your friend. I was preparing you," he retorts, as we argue over his explanation for enforcing nuclear punishment for molecular misdemeanors. Ah, yes, grasshopper, times have changed.

Today I am the ornithologist who, having spent years feeding his captive condors with a bizarre plastic hand puppet, must release them into the wild. Our drop-offs at college have become emotional pilgrimages as we take endless iPhone photographs and splash them across social media, documenting that our fledglings have arrived in their new nests. This behavior contrasts sharply with 1979, when my parents loaded up my possessions in large trash bags, and barely slowing their car down to fifteen miles per hour, shoved me out onto the curb of a blazing hot Claremont College street.

I could have sworn I heard Dad say, "Have a nice life!" My mother yelled something about not mixing coloreds and whites (she meant laundry), and my father reminded me for the millionth time of the innumerable sacrifices he had made to finance my expedition into a private college education. Within days, he had turned my bedroom into a third home office. There was no such thing as a living shrine to his collegiate children. It was his house and he was determined to retake ground lost for years to his teenaged parasites. Damn straight!

An hour after my unceremonious leave-taking, I was optimistically navigating a phalanx of young men moving toward what I thought was a keg of beer but turned out to be the only good-looking girl on our entire campus. I was on my own.

My roommate, Donald, was a circumspect academic who instantly assessed I was going to be a problem. He had arrived hours before me—with both parents. His side of the room was outfitted with a mini-refrigerator, coffee machine, photographs of his family, and a stereo system that resembled a NASA workstation. He was an only child.

After living my life among four feral boys, an insane cat, and a promiscuous dog, I was unprepared for this massive dose of personal consideration and responsibility. I was a slob, leaving a trail even Helen Keller could follow. I was Oscar to Donald's Felix. I am not sure which of us was more distressed by the fate that lashed us together. He was a soft, erudite Eloi, spending his early mornings reading the *Wall Street Journal* in the dining hall and faithfully attending 8 a.m. classes. I, on the other hand, led the sullied life of a carnivorous Morlock, laboring at night and refusing to rise before the sun had arced above the trees, which occurred around the time lunch was being served.

Over the year, the room became a collision of ideologies. One roommate was a humorless Germanesque laser-guided missile who made provisions for events that might be years away, while the other was a loud Irish skyrocket with no discernable trajectory. Donald was a genuine passive-aggressive. He would not have survived a nanosecond in the house of my father. He looked at me as if I were ten-car pile-up on the I-5 and would talk to himself when he was upset with me.

In contrast, I was a paramecium that moved only toward light, food, Grateful Dead music, and the opposite sex. I was an alien—an extraterrestrial from a universe that seemed content with chaos and the sybaritic notion that tomorrow was at least twelve hours away.

I caught him one day dressed in his church clothes. It was a Tuesday and it seemed odd that this organized Lutheran would be attending a religious service.

"Did someone die? Are you, like, going to a funeral?" I asked.

"I'm interviewing for a summer internship with Goldman Sachs." He sighed in the mirror as he looped his foulard tie under his collar.

I was perplexed. "Why would you want to work at a department store for the summer? I mean you could do much better working in a warehouse or washing windows."

He started talking to himself. "He thinks it's a department store…a department store…." He left the room. I waited a few minutes and then helped myself to some Chips Ahoy from his refrigerator and turned on an old episode of *The Twilight Zone* on his television. I laughed to myself thinking of Don working in the men's department in some lonesome mall.

I was swept away in a deluge of nostalgia as I dropped my elder son off at college this week. In many ways, he is my carbon copy, and each of his life experiences provides me with déjà vu moments of amusement. His departure has left our home with only one child remaining: me. My 16-year-old is unnervingly responsible to the point that I wonder whether he was a changeling from the hospital. There is now no one to blame for a mess or to accuse of eating the last cookies. My now-collegiate son was my air cover and my deflection. Now he is gone.

On a heavy, humid afternoon, we had lugged his bedding, lacrosse gear, clothes, and yes, coffee maker up to a pleasant two-bedroom suite. Students swirled like fireflies in blazing red shirts, flashing smiles that masked apprehension and a nervous sense of adventure. His roommate arrived: another lacrosse player and wide-eyed freshman excited to be free of his hand-puppet feeders. Once the beds were made and clothes put away, it was time to leave. The Resident Assistant stopped by to remind the boys of an orientation session while they stared out the window at a gaggle of girls confidently moving across the quad toward the cafeteria.

He seemed happy. I leaned in. "Be a good roommate," I said. "Don't be a slob. Don't waste this opportunity." I was running out of advice since most of it already had been heaped on his shoulders ad nauseam through four years of high school micromanagement.

I turned one last time. "Hey, buddy, if UBS or any of the local business guys interview on campus, let me know. You should get an interview for a summer internship."

He gave me an odd look. "Why would I want to work at a shipping company? I wanna make money. Besides, next summer is so far away."

Yep, that's my boy and I miss him.

ARISTOTLE

Aristotle and the Teenager

S ETTING: MARKET DAY, Pridi. Id. Mart (March 14), 350 BC. A sunny garden of a single family dwelling in Athens.

Plato's Academy professor Aristotle is reading a scroll while his teenaged daughter, Plecia, is scratching a rock tablet with a metal nail.

ARISTOTLE
Plecia, I want a word with you.
PLECIA
(Hammering with a chisel)
Just a minute, Father. I am finishing up this instant tablet.
(More chiseling)
There. Now, what is it, Father?
ARISTOTLE

Your mother informs me that instead of attending philosophy class today you were seen exchanging tablets with a group of teens behind the amphitheater. I have it on good authority that one of these boys was actually a Spartan.

PLEICA
(Clearly lying)

It wasn't me. I was in philosophy, and I did not go near the amphitheater during the daytime. I know the rules about going close to the rushes.

ARISTOTLE

(Raising an eyebrow)

Diogenes was wandering in the rushes and watched as the girls and boys were flirting and exchanging tablets.

PLECIA

(Looking guilty)

Diogenes? The ascetic? Why do you even talk to that wandering lunatic? He lives inside a clay jar. He never takes a bath. He walks around Athens with a lamp. In the daytime! And even if I were with Spartans, which I was not, they could teach us a thing or two about sticking up for ourselves. They're much more sophisticated than the Athenian boys, who just wrestle and discuss philosophy and logic.

ARISTOTLE

Aha! So you admit it!

PLECIA

Father, you are ruining my life. I am the only Athenian girl who doesn't have a messenger to deliver my instant tablets. Lycestra has her own scribe and her own messenger. You and mother still think it's 500 B.C. instead of 300 B.C. Wake up. You have no idea what it is like to be the daughter of a philosopher who lives in the past.

ARISTOTLE

(Looking perplexed)

First of all, Lycestra's father is an Oracle and makes many drachmae giving advice. I am a mere academic at Plato's Academy. You know I'm thinking about tutoring that Macedonian prince, but I am not in it for money.

PLECIA

(Sensing an opening)

You give everyone the impression you are so progressive with your speeches and your teaching, but you will not even allow me to go to the Pan-Hellenic Concerts at Thermopylae. You preach freedom of thought, but you keep me a prisoner. If you ask me, you are a master hypocrite.

ARISTOTLE

(Insulted)

I cannot believe you would say that. When you wanted to dye your hair green for the festival of Promethia, your mother and I agreed. You wanted a magpie as a pet and as your muse. We let you have the bird even though it defecated all over my tunic.

PLECIA

(Rolling her eyes)

Whatever.

ARISTOTLE

I told you not to use that word anymore unless you are contrasting between logical points and are uncertain of the value difference between the two. I find the term dismissive and disrespectful.

PLECIA

(Shrugging)

Okay, how about everything you say has no relevance to me, and my unfulfilled needs prevent me from relating to you on any level? If I didn't depend on you for food and shelter, I would denounce my filial relationship with you as some queer joke by Zeus and flee to Troy to become an actress in dramatic theatre.

(Stomps her foot)

I want my freedom!

ARISTOTLE

(Clasps his hands and smiles)

Fabulous. That is what I am talking about. You have been listening in humanities class. You mentioned all your necessary and possible prerequisites. You are using modal logic. While your opinions are not worthy, they are well stated.

PLEICA

(Screaming)

Father, you are not listening to me!

(Hesitates)

I have a date tonight with a Spartan named Leonidas. He has asked me to go to the Pythian wrestling matches and to dine with him afterward at the Aqueduct Grill.

ARISTOTLE

Have you gone to the public fountains for your mother to fill the goat-skin sacks with water?

PLECIA

I was going to do that later. I'm still considering whether I want to do it. I heard you tell your student the other day that it is the mark of an educated mind to be able to entertain a thought without accepting it.

ARISTOTLE

How you twist my words. I meant that you can be open to other views without accepting them. It does not mean you should avoid fulfilling your most basic of family covenants.

(The door opens.
A dwarf enters and hands the teen a tablet. The dwarf waits and looks bored as the teen smiles while reading the tablet. She hands the dwarf a new message. He leaves.)

What is this?

PLECIA

(Looking lovesick)

That was from Leonidas. I told him I would meet him when the shadows reach the steps of the amphitheater.

ARISTOTLE

If you leave this house tonight without going first to the fountain, you will be grounded for the entire Delia Festival!

PLECIA

(Under her breath)

Whatever.

ARISTOTLE

(Cringing)

There is that word again. It means nothing and torments me like a cat scratching on the wooden door of my soul.

PLECIA

(Changing tactics)

Father, how will I ever be independent unless I am allowed to make my own choices? I need a chance to make mistakes, learn, and depend upon my own thinking. Don't you tell me every day that happiness depends upon ourselves?

ARISTOTLE

(Closing eyes and reflecting)

Perhaps you have a point. But stay away from the rushes and be aware that I am going to tell Diogenes to keep an eye on you.

PLECIA

(Looking excited)

Oh, thank you, Daddy!

ARISTOTLE

So now I am Daddy?

PLECIA

Yes, and I take back everything I said. May I have forty drachmae to buy squid to throw at the winning wrestlers?

ARISTOTLE

Did I not advance your allowance through the Festival?

PLECIA

I cannot remember. Please?

(She pastes on a frozen smile.)

ARISTOTLE

Very well. But get that water from the fountains!

(He hands her coins. Plecia runs off into another part of the house. She begins furiously chiseling another message. He picks up a tablet and tries to read it. It is written in a bizarre code of half-words and acronyms. He shakes his head and puts the missive down. A magpie flies up, alights on his arm, hops up and poops on his shoulder, then flies away.)

ARISTOTLE

(Shaking his head)

The gods, too, are fond of a joke.

Christmas in Kamchatka

"I think it's wrong that only one company
makes the game Monopoly."
—STEVEN WRIGHT

COMPETITIVENESS IS LIKE a morning cowlick that never seems to settle. It pops up in the most prosaic circumstances: at the family room table across a game of Hearts as a son-in-law drops the queen of spades on his mother-in law for the third straight hand or in the sharp elbows that suddenly fly in the annual family "touch" football game. And it's in the constant skirmishes along the borders of Kamchatka during the Christmas Day game of Risk.

We like playing games in my family. I pretend not to be competitive but it is a thin veneer. The art of enjoying any contest as a type-A cutthroat adult is always to win but never let others catch you trying to win. Let them speculate on your motives but do not get caught blatantly attempting to succeed.

It is important to fake humility and to reinforce this with periodic excursions away from the game, requiring people to call you back. Forcing them to shout, "It's your turn," makes you a master of misdirection. You also must appear not to care. When crushing a 9-year-old niece in Sorry, you must seem sympathetic. "I rolled a six? Oh, I guess that means you are bumped back to home. What do you know? I win! Oh, don't cry, sweetheart. Your uncle Michael was just really lucky this time. It's only a silly game."

At family gatherings each year, the same board games appear, relics of the age of Parker Brothers, imagination, eleven-channel television sets, and computers the size of city blocks. It was the era of Monopoly, Risk, Scrabble, Parcheesi and Yahtzee. Later, we expanded our repertoire to include Pictionary and Trivial Pursuit. In fits of adult nostalgia, we repurchased these games on eBay, at yard sales, and on rainy days while on summer vacation, assuming we could vicariously recapture those magic nights through our children. Instead our children balked, bored by the games' simplicity and alarmed by our hypocrisy as we espoused sportsmanship while nonchalantly trying to force them into Chapter 11 with hotels on Illinois, Kentucky, and Indiana Avenues.

Once a year, the board games are excavated from an all-purpose storage cabinet in our family room. I am immediately on the defensive as my unimaginative teens complain about the games as too long, too monotonous, or too simple. They possess that latent American gene that screams for instant resolution and constant action.

I am difficult to beat in Risk. I am like the Chinese. While teenagers think in terms of minutes, I think in terms of hours. I fight a guerrilla war of attrition, first seizing the seemingly insignificant continent of Oceania, which comprises Australia/Indonesia. On each turn, I use the continent's two bonus armies to annoyingly pick away at anyone who tries to control Asia, Africa, or the Americas. By the time my hordes of freedom fighters have rid the last continent of my blue, green, and yellow opponents' armies, no one is paying attention. They are watching television, texting, or have left the room—indifferent Westerners bored with this protracted analog war of dice, luck, and strategy. Perhaps the next American version of Risk should include a "surge" scenario that reduces the game duration to eighteen minutes, which seems to be the maximum amount of time this generation prefers to wage war.

Monopoly holds broader appeal, although I am always forced to be the boot, which really bothers me. Others get to be the battleship, cannon, or even a Yorkshire terrier. I am convinced the boot is jinxed, as I can never seem to land on Boardwalk when it is free to be purchased. The boot usually lands on the luxury tax space until someone has built a hotel on Park Place, and then it seems happy to pay $1,500 for a shoeshine.

There are two types of Monopoly players—Main Street and Wall Street. Wall Streeters buy everything, make deals, and forge alliances. They mortgage their own properties to raise more money to buy more properties and build more hotels. They are always one roll of the dice from bankruptcy. They consider themselves too big to fail. These risk-addicted individuals take on maximum leverage and seek to create a bubble that will pop in the face of their Main Street opponent.

Main Street is cautious but naïve. They buy properties like Mediterranean and Vermont Avenues because it is cheap to build hotels. Main Street buys utilities and railroads. Against the advice of armchair observers, Main Street trustingly trades Park Place to Wall Street for $1,000 cash, Connecticut Ave., and three free "lands." An hour later, Main Street has mortgaged his last property and is begging for one more turn so he might pass Go and avoid losing his racecar. Wall Street crushes him like a cigarette butt.

In our house, my opponents are subject to constant third party coaching from in-laws and do-gooders who do not want to risk competing but loiter like homeless people and shamelessly kibitz. "Watch out for your dad," shouts my mother-in-law. "Don't do that deal, sweetie," my wife says to my son. "Don't you see in one hour, you will land on Park Place and owe him everything?" I look up with a frozen perfunctory grin. "Who are you people, regulators?" I ask. "Don't you have homes? Or perhaps some Christmas cards to write?"

My bloodthirsty competitiveness was born out of a third-child struggle for attention in a four-child ecosystem. Competition was everywhere and my father did not attempt to defuse it. He correctly assumed that the younger would struggle more fiercely and in doing so perhaps be that much more braced for what lay ahead in the great oceans of life.

Mercy did not exist during the games played in our male-dominated household. Games taught us valuable life skills such as the game face, blackmail, extortion, and intimidation. Each Christmas competition was a page torn from Sun Tzu's *The Art of War*. "Be extremely subtle, even to the point of formlessness. Be extremely mysterious, even to the point of soundlessness. Thereby you can be the director of the opponent's fate."

My brother, Tom, owned me in all games and was the master of blackmail and misinformation. He understood when Sun Tzu mused, "The supreme art of war is to subdue the enemy without fighting." He could make me choke faster than a large piece of filet mignon. I can remember that fateful Christmas when I finally prevailed over him at Risk. As I harassed his pitiful armies across North America to a last stand in Greenland, I understood the sense of power of Alexander, Genghis Kahn, and Caesar. On this night, I was master of the universe.

Later, Trivial Pursuit and Pictionary tested our left and right brains. Trivial Pursuit is more daunting and clearly creates social and generational barriers. As a sports, history, literature, and movie buff, I can adequately vie for two-thirds of the pie wedges. However, I am lost in geography and without Bunsen burner in science. Trivial Pursuit has produced a variety of themed versions that garner more attention from younger family members. However, the popular culture version has about as much appeal to me as a regular culture: a Petri dish of wriggling micro-celebrity parasites who will only infect and weaken society. If you ever catch me playing a game where "Kim Kardashian" is an answer to anything, please kill me.

Pictionary is very frustrating. As an artist, I am outraged when my wife's Pictionary partner correctly interprets that her Neanderthal hieroglyphic represents "global warming," while my impatient teammate is screaming out names of countries as I try to correctly draw the Horn of Africa on my brilliant rendition of the earth. My pedestrian theory is that Pictionary was invented by the legions of the artistically challenged that wanted to get back at their more talented right-brained siblings. Pictionary is hell.

Card games such as hearts, poker, gin rummy, and bridge all afford opportunities for reprisals, heckling, and old-fashioned spirited competition, and as the last card falls, the final property flips into foreclosure, or the final pie piece is won, the combatants heave a great sigh. Arms stretch and a slow migration occurs, usually to the refrigerator as the vanquished look to food for solace and comfort. The game accouterments are collected and carefully returned to their boxes. It will be another year before we again do battle. However, there are really no losers. We have huddled together once again like all families since the beginning of time. A tiny human tribe—loving, fragile and imperfect—drawn together by competition and the chance, perhaps, to proclaim ourselves ruler of the holiday.

Living with the Lost Boys

"All children, except one, grow up."
—J.M. Barrie, *Peter Pan*

THE SUDDEN PIVOT in the meteorologist's forecast was highly displeasing. Having already missed an opportunity for a white Christmas, I was now fixated on our imminent four-day mini-break to Orlando, where we would enjoy some old-fashioned family time with our increasingly oversubscribed teenagers.

Boxing Day was spent sluggishly cleaning up from Christmas and nervously watching the Weather Channel as the predictions of a winter nor'easter were confirmed. A perfect storm of airline-emasculating zero-visibility winds and tarmac-snarling snow had descended over the entire region. With three-foot snowfalls predicted to entomb the area I finally understood why native Northeasterners loathe the romantic notion of a late December snowstorm. The woods may be lovely, dark and deep, but snow means no flight out to find some heat.

Our flight had an ETD of 6 a.m. Monday, during the peak of the storm. The question was not whether our flight would be delayed, but whether we would be able to book a later flight once the airline came clean and canceled our morning escape to Florida.

At 11 a.m. Sunday morning, Flight 987 was officially cancelled. The 800 number provided by the airline was overwhelmed to a point that any ticket-holder tenacious enough to cling to the queue was being asked to try back later—and then unceremoniously dropped from the call. Logistical certainty was in short supply on this day. We continued to badger the airline to determine if a late Monday or early Tuesday departure might salvage our best-laid plans.

After finessing our way to a customer service operator (I do not recall how we found this trap door; perhaps we indicated we had special needs), we were told that we could get five tickets to Orlando late Wednesday evening or early Thursday morning. The understanding agent did not seem to divine that this new itinerary would afford us less than forty-eight hours in the Sunshine State. Given that thirty of those hours would be either dark or with temperatures less than fifty degrees, I was skeptical of a decent return on investment.

The agent offered to reschedule our return, but this would require rebooking the tickets for an additional $150 penalty per ticket. I did some quick napkin calculus and determined this vacation would cost us around $100 for each hour of potential sunshine. I could save $3,500 if I bought everyone his or her own jar of Vitamin D and three free sessions at the Savage Tropic tanning salon.

We euthanized our vacation late Boxing Day afternoon. Our teens temporarily mourned the passing of our trip the way one might lament the death of a distant relative. After five minutes of self-reflection, they shifted their attention to the living and began rapidly pinging their friends for sleepovers, parties, and any other forms of nocturnal activity.

My wife would require more time to recover from our vacation's sudden cardiac arrest. She was facing the grim reality of an entire week with a thoughtless quartet of the undead—creatures of the night who would conspire to overrun her best efforts to keep a clean house and avoid endless meal preparation and hourly carpools.

As a stay-at-home vacation dad, I am at best a weak surrogate and at worst a human sinkhole of mixed messages that undermine my family's carefully negotiated routines and boundaries regarding curfews, chores, and accountability.

Instead of pushing everyone to bed at an early hour for our pre-dawn vacation departure, we stayed up until 2 a.m. playing poker and watching old movies. Our cancelled flight allowed us to dive into a week of freshly fallen snow and a clear calendar. However, I took the cue from my teenagers and began the slow transformation into a vampire.

My first mistake was suggesting the X-Box 360 be moved upstairs from the basement into the family room so we could enjoy a big-screen version of FIFA soccer, NCAA football, Tony Hawk Underground, and of course, the culturally enriching Call of Duty: Black Ops.

Most of my black ops activities are confined to eating unhealthy food late at night and making frivolous purchases on eBay. However, I was now being recruited into an adolescent band of brothers whose motto was "Leave no man behind—alive." Aside from their annoying habit of shooting me in the back for sport, my boys drew me into hours of constant violence in some of the poorest nations around the globe. While learning how to operate an automatic Famas gun, throw a ballistic knife, and detonate crossbow explosives, I was beginning to show signs of PTSD.

Later that evening, my wife realized the open week was not trending in her favor. As she laid down the holiday rules and regulations (she had just discovered that the dog had urinated by the door because none of us had noticed his whimpering), I stood by her side with genuine disdain for my teens. "Look guys, Mom is right. You need to pull your weight around here."

She turned and looked at me incredulously. "Really?"

Falling in with these slacker vampires had been so easy. It was reminiscent of college: late nights, sleeping in until noon, occasionally venturing out to a movie, ordering in, and groaning with exaggerated inconvenience when asked to do anything that had nothing in it for me. It was an amazingly rapid metamorphosis from parent to parasite.

Two days into my Twilight regression, I had a moment of clarity. I glanced up to survey a hoarder's landscape of squalor—Cheez-It and Goldfish boxes, empty bottles of Diet Coke, and played-out Nutri-Grain wrappers. The evening before, I had stayed up until 3 a.m. to finally defeat my eldest son in a barn burner football game that went into double overtime. The dog was asleep on the couch while two other teens sat in a digital stupor on separate computers watching reruns of *Modern Family* on Hulu.

To the shock of my fellow primates, I pushed the "save" button on my latest game of NCAA Football. I was now into my third season of the Dynasty segment of NCAA Football 2011. While no longer a contributing member of society, I was, however, virtual head coach of the USC Trojans. I had also developed an almost stenographer-type dexterity with my fingers, using what felt like twelve digits to work every A – Z button on the controller.

My son glanced up. "Dad, where are you going? You just unlocked a new level in your game." A new level? I thought. I was suddenly very afraid that if I descended deeper into this artificial gridiron matrix, I might never return. I had to escape from the underworld and find my way to the surface of the living—and I had to leave right now.

I showered and shaved, glancing at the unimpressive image of a pale Baby Boomer with bloodshot eyes. I emerged into the crisp air and sunshine of a gorgeous winter afternoon determined to drive—anywhere. My car seemed to guide me into town, where the sidewalks were likely to be alive with adults and responsible people, others who perhaps had missed their flights or did not live in a sarcophagus of teens.

Suddenly, I spied my wife's car and spotted her moving slowly down the street, probably window-shopping for post-holiday bargains or a family practice attorney. "Hey," I said breathlessly as I caught up to her. She was pleased to see I had escaped the iron grip of the Lost Boys. We lingered over a latte-fueled lunch and made plans for the New Year.

The afternoon yielded to purple twilight. The streets were emptying. The human beings were slowly returning home to prepare meals, read books, rest by a fire, and contemplate the next days and all of their possibilities.

A knot of new shadows appeared outside our café window. Six young vampires wearing hooded cotton sweatshirts, shorts, and high-top sneakers were rolling restlessly across the frigid street. They had all temporarily abandoned their computers and X-Boxes to roam the town in search of a source of entertainment.

I felt a call of the wild stir as I surveyed the aimless, rudderless spill of hormones splashing onto the sidewalk. They would soon end up at a new safe house, retreating by the light of day, waiting for another nervous night. My phone buzzed and a message appeared from the world of adults: a misguided colleague choosing to work the graveyard slot between Christmas and New Year's. I put away the iPhone and returned to my partner and our plans.

I smiled, realizing I hadn't made a very good vampire for years. Vampires did not understand the difference between living in the moment and living as if there were no tomorrow. Vampires consider the past an empty bucket of ashes, the present an endless horizon-line road, and the future as something that happens to other people.

My wife and I were thinking about the future, about the New Year and things we needed to do to make a difference. I felt my chin, freshly cleared of a forty-eight-hour goatee of vampire stubble.

They had almost pulled me into their red-pill world of artificial intelligence and the insatiable craving for constant distraction, but I had survived my time with the Lost Boys. As I sipped my coffee, I wondered how it was possible that I survived the purgatory of my own youth. For all of its challenges and responsibilities, it was good to be above ground and among the mortals ready to take on another year.

Once upon a Redecoration

"Beige is atmosphere. It's bisque, it's ivory, it's cream, it's stone, it's toast, it's cappuccino. It's, well, it's magic." Adam Lewis

SPRING IS HERE, or at least it has been rumored to be skirting our area. I notice a stirring and restless, frenetic activity in the woods as another generation of flora and fauna stretches into the longer days of April. Resurrection is in the air and repair everywhere—stone walls, gutters, and roofs damaged by a bloated winter whose derriere squatted longer and harder on the Northeast than in years past.

A charm of finches flits across my garden, frantically engrossed in gathering twigs, while plump, red-breasted robins patrol my lawn. It seems every living thing is rousing out of the stupor of an endless night of winter days. It is a happy, serotonin-fueled time for new resolutions and projects. Change is in the air.

It is also at this time of year that other nest builders begin to itch for change. The warning signs are subtle and hard to differentiate from the normal cadence of spring-cleaning. Only the trained eye of a veteran husband can detect the overactive imaginations, the incessant daydreaming, and indefatigable minds of women as the lighter days inspire them to reconsider the interior designs of their homes.

It begins with an almost undetectable dog-eared page in *House Beautiful* and quickly escalates to the discovery of *Connecticut Homes* stuffed between the mattresses like a forbidden girlie magazine. These periodicals are the gateway drugs to an eventual addiction to home improvement television shows followed by long "shopping" trips from which my partner returns with no purchased item other than some benign pieces of fabric and a few innocent-looking colored placards similar in size to Candyland cards. The next thing you know, some New York City metrosexual named RicKi (yes, a capital K) is in my living room declaring it a candidate for FEMA fashion relief.

I recall watching my mother gush every time she would visit the homes of friends and neighbors with older children. She would stare at my father as she flattered our hosts on their choices of fabrics and décor. Years later, I realized her praise was laced with anger and envy. Raising destructive boys and a dog that preferred to urinate on the corner of her living room sofa had left her paralyzed, not even able to attempt a home makeover.

My freshman-year of college, a woman who could be best described as the unholy offspring of Rodney Dangerfield and Phyllis Diller arrived at our front door. She was a prominent Beverly Hills interior designer who was doing a friend a favor by agreeing to meet with my mother, aka "that poor woman with the four boys."

"My gaaaawd! Honey, I don't know how you have survived so long living in GI Joe's footlocker. I mean, it looks like Burt Reynolds threw up all over your house!" Her hysterical laugh quickly yielded to a smoker's cough that sounded as if she might hack up a fur ball. My mother could respond only with a nervous, embarrassed chuckle. She shot my father the "lizard look"—a squinting leer that silently conveyed more contempt than any combination of words in the Merriam-Webster dictionary.

The auburn bombshell proceeded into our living room, surveying its sculpted olive-green shag carpet; overstuffed, urine-stained twin floral sofas; and a bamboo wall-to-wall stereo cabinet that seemed better suited to a potting shed. My dad was not sure whether this woman was a homemaker or a home wrecker, as it was clear that he was about to take the rap for my mother's sudden epiphany that she had been living a life of squalor.

Overnight, our comfortable *Father Knows Best* living room transformed into a sterile showcase home fit only for women, demure young girls, and clients. An entire living space in our home became off-limits and remained unoccupied for weeks on end. Any living thing with hair under its arms was relegated to a postage-stamp-sized den. To add insult to injury, my father was required to compensate this domestic fashionista. He eventually came to refer to her simply as "the parasite," a generous sobriquet ascribed to anyone who diverted resources or attention away from his needs.

Currently, a strange woman keeps leaving messages for my wife on our machine. She talks rapidly and always in code. "Hi, Caroline, I've got those swatches you were asking about and will leave them in the store for you." Swatches? I am suddenly aware of little pieces of laminated colored paper taped to the living room wall.

The beige and powder-blue squares have names like "healing aloe" and "soft fern." The soft fern color is actually light gray, which looks more like "dead fern" to me. Other squares of Sherwin-Williams paint are perfumed and lipsticked with names such as "deer path" and "baby's breath." Personally, all I think of when I see those overheated descriptions are round pebbles of scat and curdled milk.

I actually have not met the happy interior design lady. I can visualize her as she parades across my perfectly acceptable living and family rooms with that puzzled, sympathetic look of a cosmetic surgeon. "Has it always looked this way? Personally, I can see why you don't want a cluttered feel to the room."

"Cluttered" is female-speak for everything I find comfortable. Clutter will be banished to the basement.

As the home makeover escalates, it becomes physically inconvenient. It requires me to move stuff. I hate moving stuff. A call from another room is a colossal imposition. "Hon, I need you to hold this mirror up for me," or "Can you move that 500-pound urn over to that corner? I just want to see how it looks." At the whim of my spouse and the invisible furniture muse, I become a thankless Druid rebuilding Stonehenge slab by slab each night. One particularly irksome request has me moving everything on the right side of the room to the left side and vice versa. Other than potentially accommodating some ancient principle of feng shui, I can see no purpose to this exercise other than turning my L1 through L5 vertebrae into a ruptured, gelatinous kebab.

My vigorous plyometrics continue nightly. "A little higher. No, higher. No, lower. Just two inches to the right." The 200-pound mirror is about to smash to the ground as I near muscle failure. She hesitates. I crane my neck and encourage this new location. Actually, at this point, I would endorse its relocation anywhere, including the garage. "Nope," she says, shaking her head. "It's not quite right." The mirror plunges and I stick out my shoe to protect it from hitting the floor. It crushes my toe. I swear and hop on one leg. Her back is turned. "Let's try it over here," she says.

As I limp to bed that night, I have vivid nightmares of my house being overrun with green alpaca-fiber bunny-rabbit-themed throws and emerald Fabergé eggs. An orange man with a feather boa keeps trying to convince me that the latest design style is to have an empty room where everyone just stands.

I wake up in a cold sweat and stumble into the kitchen. As I pass through the darkened living room, I can see swatches of fabric draped over the arms of chairs and sofas. The décor demon has passed this way again. When will this end? Will it begin with a reupholstered chair and conclude with my wife telling me she needs a divorce because my eyes don't match the new living room carpet? I turn on a light and mindlessly open one of a thousand décor magazines littering the coffee table—the latest issue of *Dwell*.

I can't help feeling cynical. I mean, who the hell buys *Dwell* magazine anyway? Who writes for *Dwell*? Interior design people who can't make up their minds? I open the smartly illustrated cover and an article catches my eye: "Man Caves." The hunting lodge theme encourages dark wood accents, such as bookshelves, and rich mahogany furniture. The article patronizingly concludes with, "Don't forget, men need simplicity, so avoid clutter." (There's that code word again). I survey the chocolate-brown leather chairs, the floor to ceiling bookcase, the crown molding and midnight slate fireplace. This would make a good man cave.

In a moment of self-serving clarity, I realize I must actively participate in this remodel lest I awaken one day to a family room transformed into a day spa with the stereo piping out New Age Peruvian pan-pipe music. I fold the page, marking the article on hunting-lodge man caves and slip the magazine underneath my wife's pillow.

It's my turn now.

Unplugged and Out West

"You can't take highways during the apocalypse,
because they'll be packed with panicky people."
—J. Cornell Michel, *Jordan's Brains: A Zombie Evolution*

EACH YEAR, OUR family swims like salmon against a current of temporal obligations and fights to return to the calm, sun-sequined rivers of my West Coast youth. We always arrive conflicted—barraged by the need to see family and old friends, but at the same time wanting to immerse ourselves in this massive, self-obsessed amusement park called California.

I am always nervous returning to Los Angeles, as every email I receive from my father suggests that his once Golden State has declined into a dystopian cesspool where rampant illegal immigration, corrupt public officials, profligate public spending, and fewer public restrooms have made it unfit for working people, the elderly, and those with prostate issues.

My West Coast past and East Coast present are two distinct worlds, and I worry when they collide. The stories of my youthful mischief have been hidden like state secrets that must incubate in silence for at least seventy-five years. The risk in coming west is that we will encounter a long-lost acquaintance who will proceed to tell one of my children, "Your father, oh, he was a wild thing!" This opens a Pandora's Box of interrogation I find increasingly hard to navigate.

As my digital-age children get older, the logistics of our time together are complicated by their own predictable canyons of self-absorption and technology. They are like single-bar cellular calls that often drop unbeknownst to the speaker. One can spend minutes talking, unaware that the other party is no longer on the line.

"I'm sorry, Dad, I lost you after you said, 'Will you please'..." is followed by the always irritating "I'm sorry, I don't speak Spanish" expression.

The family road trip has radically morphed since the days of "Shut up or I'll give you something to complain about" automobile travel. In the '70s, our family was a predictable part of a summer land rush of urban and suburban families, enthusiastically driving to a vacation destination and establishing ourselves for a week like a hive of yellow jackets. We would normally infest some sad rental beach house or motel and find things to do. "I'm bored," was always met with, "Go outside and don't come back until dinnertime."

Among the things found to do were some that were legal and some that weren't. But invariably we would return to our home base for food, medical attention, zinc oxide, or with the feral dog we had just found and wanted to keep.

Comfortable mini-SUVs have replaced the Fleetwood wagon and its Russian-cattle-car seating arrangements. A grand bazaar of roadside fast food chains has supplanted warm Shasta sodas and bleeding Wonder Bread PBJs we greedily devoured at highway picnic areas. If we were ever to visit a rest stop today, my kids would assume we were stopping to dump a dead body.

"I want a Jamba Juice, Dad."

"We're in the middle of the California desert, buddy. There's nothing here but sand and horizon-line highway."

"Well, actually, I just Yelped Jamba Juice and there is one in Victorville. It's only five miles off the freeway on a frontage road, and it's near an In-N-Out Burger." Cheers erupt from the trio of back seat drivers, and within minutes we are eating double-double cheeseburgers under a high-desert neon sign.

The American meal has kept pace with our soaring national debt, with portions eclipsing the size of a Central American banana republic. To combat the disease of oversized portions, we assign a "designated scavenger" at each meal. The scavenger does not order any food but may sample from any and all plates.

Since she is the smallest and least selfish, my spouse often assumes this role, believing that food tastes better when it comes off other people's plates. As a child of Brits who survived the London blitz, she is genetically predisposed to be a scavenger. We estimate ordering for four instead of five saves between fifteen and twenty percent on meals, impedes inevitable holiday weight gain, and modestly improves the mileage on our fossil-fuel-guzzling Sherman Tank of an SUV.

The once-almighty twentieth-century automobile pilgrimage replete with its sibling battles, carsickness, and endless boredom has been tenderized by satellite radio, personal entertainment systems, instant messaging, and ubiquitous Wi-Fi coverage. My children have been reduced to digital cocoons. No one listens or looks as my wife and I describe the rugged beauty and history of California's eastern Sierra and Owens Valley.

While we might be together on vacation, it is a rare harmonic convergence when we are all emotionally present. The digital age has broken the nuclear family into pieces; we are isolated microbytes of data symbiotically sharing a common ecosystem called a house. Each day the family must compete with alternative communities: enemy cells of friends via Live Chat, a conveyor belt of Snapchat photographs, and a mindless sewage pipe of text messages.

We arrive at our mountain destination and a late dinner at a crowded restaurant. The entire establishment is also suffering from digital cocooning, with three out of four patrons slumped at the altars of their glowing handheld devices and smart phones. I assume everyone is texting or making PowerPoint presentations to one another.

There is one loud table. It is a group of five men and women who are actually talking and joking. People glare at them with scorn. It seems so rude that they should be making noise in this dining place where no one speaks. Sadly, the digital pollution drift has invaded the last bastion where table manners, grammar, syntax, and personal mythology are passed on—the family dinner table.

I conjure up the countenance of my T-Rex father and growl at the children, explaining that I am capable of extinguishing them if they do not extinguish their devices. You would think I'd asked them to give CPR to an anthropophage. I suggest a trivia game where we might stimulate our minds. My son protests, "How can we play trivia if we can't look up the answers on Chrome?"

"Name five famous people whose first or last names are a color."

Feeling clever, I eagerly await their answers. I can see the encouraging signs of nascent collaboration.

"Pink," my daughter says, shrugging. "Can we use our phones now?"

"No, damn it! I want four more." They look as if I had asked them to explain the Fibonacci Sequence.

"Who was the coach of the Boston Celtics? Who played football for Syracuse and the Browns? Who starred in *Nacho Libre* and *School of Rock*? Okay, here's a hint. What about the names with "Red," "Brown," or "Black?""

"Oh, I know," yells one of the boys. "Red Brown."

"Who is that?" I ask.

"I don't know, wasn't he like a football coach? I should get two points for that!"

I shake my head and to my wife's chagrin regress into off-color jokes and potty humor as a lowest-common-denominator method of keeping our conversation afloat.

It is indeed harder each year to be an analog parent in a digital world that so empowers the individual. The road-trip holiday continues to meet stiff headwinds as our young adults become addicted to the instant gratification and entertainment of omnipresent media. The notion of down time is tantamount to prison time, with the definition of fun having changed into the need for 24/7 distraction.

My learned behavior of working as a team arose out of our family's Bataan Death March childhood vacations and our common circumstances: the tedium of long car rides; the inconvenience of being torn from the moorings of friends; and roadside Bates motels with creepy proprietors, toxic, chlorinated pools, and no television.

Each summer we were forced to hang out as a family and amuse one another. We were unplugged and managed by unfiltered, orthodox parents. They told us to eat all of our food because children were starving in China. We now are concerned our kids are eating too much and that China is no longer starving.

For the twentieth-century vacation, each kid saved money for the annual road trip to places such as the Grand Canyon so we might buy a magical vial of Painted Desert sand or a sinister scorpion encased inside a paperweight. Today it seems we are constantly looking for a store that sells iPhone power cords. Travel was about seeing new places and punching holes in the walls of our suburban cocoons. During the new millennium, however, each person is a self-contained Bose home theatre. As we move along the blue highways of our country, it seems we are lost not in America but in cyberspace.

"Are we there yet?" has been replaced by, "Where the hell are we and will they have Wi-Fi?" Twentieth-century parents are becoming part of a new slang whose meaning we don't yet understand. We are middle-aged pragmatists who have seen too much but are lashed to the mast with young immortals who believe bad things happen only to other people. We will forever disagree on whether tomorrow is guaranteed. We have evolved as a modern family unit, and it will fall to sociologists and our descendants to determine whether we have regressed or progressed as responsible stewards of our tribes.

My spouse and I now seek vacation destinations that lack cell service: remote locales and pristine back roads where our digital progeny are forced to notice the tumbling streams, alpine lakes, and rock-strewn paths lined with purple lupine and blood-red Indian paintbrush. On today's hike, my daughter spots an almost-invisible mother deer and her spotted fawn navigating a steep brown hillside of talus. At home, this same daughter can barely make out a stop sign. We watch and stand quietly at a forty-five-degree angle before the deer melt into a stand of pines at the timberline. We stop for lunch and break out books or just meditate, absorbing the grandeur of this glacial basin reflected in an emerald-green lake.

I am convinced that our biology requires us to be upright and outdoors. We are not constructed to sit behind desks with our vertebrae compressed and our abdominal muscles atrophying by the minute. Evolution has not yet come to a firm conclusion, but our activities might eventually turn us into human thumbs with massive derrieres and no peripheral vision. Today's hike, designed to reverse this trend, will take all day, covering eight miles and two thousand feet of elevation gained and lost.

I help set up fishing rods and devour a half-sandwich, which after three hours in my pack appears to have been the seat cushion for a circus fat lady. I chase it down with water I have just filtered from a stream.

"Hey, I got a fish!" my son yells. I rush over to extract the treble-hook lure from the oversized mouth of a speckled golden-and-red-bellied brook trout. In the harsh and desolate grasp of the high alpine climate, the fish cannot get enough nourishment. Yet they adapt and thrive because they are wild and often healthier than their corpulent brethren raised on Power Bait handouts in the captivity of a state-run hatchery.

As the sun retreats below a 14,000-foot peak, we estimate we have two hours of light left to navigate the four miles of switchbacks down to the parking area at the base of Bishop Creek, where we initiated our day. We are unplugged, enjoying a simpler, sweeter kind of music. These moments are gentle notes from a five-string guitar. We joke and gently disparage each other's shortcomings—our limitations magnified by proximity, the day's physical challenges, and the absence of creature comforts.

I begin to retell the tales of my family and these sacred places, and the times that shaped this part of America like the winds and glaciers that dominate the landscape. I am trailing the group and yelling ahead to them, talking to no one in particular. I am proud of my ability to wrench them out their routines and put them in touch with their more durable alter egos.

I notice someone has a single white strand of wire surreptitiously falling between his hair and his backward facing baseball cap. My son seems to be moving, but not to the rhythm of the story of how ignominious Convict Lake got its name. He is clearly advancing to the cadenced percussion of a band called Phoenix. More earplugs appear, and my wife and I are once again alone. She smiles. "It was nice while it lasted."

Like everything in nature, unplugged passages soon fade. They are ephemeral—a fish rising in the early morning light, leaving only green-sequined circles of water. They are a night canopy of stars, unpolluted by the distant light of cities and material obligations. The sky is an unexplained ocean where satellites move like distant cargo ships and meteors course past the corners of our eyes with sudden streaks of light.

Only the earth and sky are permanent. I recognize that my children's cocoons are temporary. They exist for a short time in this insular chrysalis that forms and protects them until a butterfly can emerge and fly away. For a moment, I can see them through the gossamer threads—moving, jostling, evolving, and changing.

A blue jay scolds me as I take one last look at the valley below. My legs hurt and my body is reminding me of my mortality. Yet I have made it once again to this special place: the high palisades of my youth, the mountains that required my full attention and commanded respect. They underscore my insignificance but reinforce the notion that I am part of something divine.

My son stops and takes a picture of the valley and the deeply shadowed, late-afternoon peaks. He stops and peers at his photograph. He smiles. The memory memorialized, it soon will be distributed to five hundred followers who will participate on an endless digital social comment thread.

The first comment arrives: "Dude, where are you? That place looks wicked."

It is. It's really cool.

A Fractured History of the Promenade

"Telling a teenager the facts of life is like giving a fish a bath."
—ARNOLD H. GLASOW

T IS A night unlike any other in America. It is twelve hours of paradox, with a generation of helicopter pilots taking ten thousand digital photographs of early-blooming debutantes escorted by young men who appear not to have conquered puberty. While fathers pout and quietly pine for a second chance at adolescence, mothers return home to hold a candlelight vigil, praying to God that this annual fusion of immaturity and immortality will not end in disaster. Across town at the local Italian Center, another generation will dive headlong into a mosh pit of tuxedoed kings and gowned queens eager to erase eighteen years of privation. It is prom night.

Prom is a seminal life event for most American teens. For some, the memory of a prom is a private scar or missed opportunity. For others, it is a wistful breeze of emotion that floats in on the scent of a gardenia.

Most academics contend the origin of the prom is British and relates simply to the concept of the promenade—a long parade of guests who would enter a ballroom or gathering area at the beginning of a social event. Escorts and debutantes would arrive in six-horse carriages, the nineteenth-century equivalent of a stretch limo, to socialize and dance. It was a patrician affair where participants would exhibit their breeding and etiquette, and possibly end the evening donning a Victorian lampshade for a few cheap laughs.

Anthropologists dismiss Anglophiles' claims that the United Kingdom was the epicenter of the prom. Researchers have traced the first prom back to the Pleistocene and the lower Paleolithic periods when the first humans walked the planet. The term "prom" was actually a collective noun used to describe a gathering of mixed-gendered adolescent *Homo erectus*.

Reconstructing these gatherings has proven difficult, as the teens seemed to gather in one place and then move unpredictably, usually to the leeward side of a granite outcrop or copse of trees. "We surmise," muses Timothy Pimthwaite of the London Anthropological Society, "that these proms of juvenile hominoids would gather, secrete some sort of pheromone that would in turn arouse the group and attract more hominoids, causing a frenzied series of interactions and mating behaviors. Within minutes, the groups would move out of sight of the adults, as if hiding or experimenting with brief independence. The youth would seek protective cover from prominent landmarks in caves and thickets. A few industrious ones even climbed trees. What they were doing has never been documented."

It was in a shaded glen of elms near the celebrated caves in Altamira, France that a British anthropologist encountered discarded hollowed-out gourds that male researchers assumed were primitive cups that held some sort of nectar. One female researcher, who also happened to be a mother of five teenagers, quickly surmised that these were in fact, the first Stone Age beer cans.

Researchers theorize that the formal pairing of adolescents to celebrate prom as "dates" was a relatively recent phenomenon dating back to the 1890s when British men got tired of attending dances with other British men, as no self-respecting Victorian woman would actually be seen dancing with any beneath her social standing. This was also the golden age of British pantomimes, in which male actors would dress up as women to entertain audiences with silly skits and stories. Given that Queen Victoria resembled a man made all of this same-gender activity remarkably good form.

However, it took a nudge from the continent to move the Brits off of same-sex proms. The first *formal* coed prom took place in the Austro-Hungarian

Alsace in 1914. The teenage graduation party was a smashing success. Unfortunately, many of the youths got drunk at a local Hofbräuhaus and in a fit of patriotic fervor, the boys and girls carried their party into neighboring France and occupied a French village for a week, escalating tensions between the Hungarian Empire and France. A week later, a Serbian shopkeeper whose windows had been broken in the post-party melee shot Archduke Franz Ferdinand, whose son was one of the offending vandals, sparking WWI. It seems even then kids did not understand the consequences of their actions and adults ended up footing the bill.

The prom disappeared for a few years as most kids graduated and were immediately sent off to Flanders to fight. For a few years, only girls and flat-footed deaf men were attending proms. In 1919, the prom entered its golden age, as returning soldiers and high school sweethearts were reunited in church halls to give thanks for the end of the global conflict. The prom became a dignified and respectful affair, with ballroom dancing, fruit punch, and prayer. Other than the occasional Catholic sneaking into an Anglican church to spike the punch or bribe the bandleader to play "The Vatican Rag," things moved rather smoothly into the early twentieth century.

In the '20s, the prom became immensely popular among elite colleges and finishing schools. In industrial America, most teens bypassed higher education to work and, as a result, the prom went private. In the era of F. Scott Fitzgerald and Jay Gatsby, tuxedos and fashionable gowns gained a foothold, transforming the tame puritanical dance into a patrician orgy of celebration. It was during this decade that teens started to wear increasingly outrageous ensembles as a form of misguided self-expression. This unfortunate period is now classified as the "dark age of fashion," and at its nadir the purple tuxedo was born.

Proms carried on. There were triumphs and tragedies as generations gathered for a fraction of a lifetime—one night—and then went off to college, work, wars, and distant hard lives that would carve deep lines in the faces of these young adults so full of life. There were auto accidents and drug overdoses compelling parents to abandon their anxiety-ridden vigils to proactively help shape the evening's festivities so that the youngsters might enjoy their rite of passage but not end up a grisly prop on some traffic safety film called, Red Asphalt.

Fifty years later in the '70s, there would be nostalgic revival of late '20s fashion fiascos. In one instance, critics described a black polyester and chiffon gown as fit only for someone "dressing like a centerfold for *Farmer's Almanac* magazine" and abused another rhinestone ensemble as a "truck-stop fashion tragedy." Combining these sartorial train wrecks with mullet and feathered hairstyles hijacked the prom into a new territory. It was no longer a tradition to be meticulously honored but a generational rite of self-expression.

Certain accouterments have survived the years of metamorphosis. The fragrant corsage and the boutonniere known as the "man flower" remain important accessories even into the twenty-first century. The prom is now a well-oiled machine for which communities and parents organize to build safe environments where teens can roam and forge a personal album of memories. Text messaging, cell phones, and electronics have supplanted word of mouth, massive amplifiers, speakers, and the telephone trees of overly paranoid parents.

Yet time waits for no man. Each prom, like Dickens' Ghost of Christmas Present, has a life span of twelve hours. The early morning light enters somewhere off in the distance like a theatre cleaning crew reminding the actors and actresses that their passion play is concluding. A young man sits exhausted as his date lays her head on his shoulder and falls asleep. The smell of her perfumed hair and warmth of her breath on his neck stir a restless flutter that grows and seeks to express itself—out of his body, out of his town, and beyond his adolescence.

The promenade is a swirl of lights, a merry-go-round of time and motion. The chrysalis breaks with the dawn and the butterflies are released. They float off into the morning mist graceful and invincible. Some may not return to this place. Others will faithfully return like swallows every five years to remember.

Yes, it was the prom and it was their time.

A Farewell Kiss to Miss Crystal

"If animals could speak, the dog would be a blundering outspoken fellow; but the cat would have the rare grace of never saying a word too much."
—Mark Twain

THE DOCTOR STUDIED the malignant shadows on Crystal's lungs as the weak arc of winter sun was devoured by denuded trees. Amidst these winter solstice days, the world is trapped in permanent twilight.

Her breathing had been labored for the past few days and she had stopped eating. "I really can't tell if the fluid is from some type of heart failure or a mass in her chest," he remarked absentmindedly as he turned the x-ray image sideways. "We probably need an EKG. She's an old lady and well, these things happen. I suppose we can refer you to an oncologist, but if it is a mass, you might do well to start thinking about making arrangements."

Arrangements?

"She could be in pain. There's no way of knowing at this point until we drain the fluid and try to see what's causing it. It's not good, though. For now, take her home and try to keep her comfortable."

Is there not a Sloan Kettering for cats?

It had been a long day, and I was not emotionally prepared for a dinner discussion about palliative care, hospice, or Dr. Kevorkian. This was not just any cat. This was Crystal—she-wolf of the pachysandra, eviscerator of raptors and rodents, and my literary muse. The vet seemed not to notice that his suggestion was asking our family to euthanize a section of our own hearts.

My wife looked as though she had been on the losing side of a Mike Tyson fight. Her swollen eyes betrayed a heartbroken day she spent on the edge of the bed stroking the gaunt, aging lioness whose purr still thrummed like a 350-horsepower engine.

It all hit me, the sepia flood of pet memories: a cavalcade of cats, dogs, fish, turtles, newts, snakes, hamsters, rats —all taken by automobiles, old age, ignorance, disease, other pets, and in one case, a cannibalistic sibling, a crime scene that still ranked in my mind with the Tate and LaBianca murders. There was never time for emotional preparation; we would return home from school only to be told of Frank the alligator lizard's untimely demise. We would mourn life's cruel inequities. The death often would be followed by a memorial worthy of a head of state. We would carefully line a shoebox coffin, often with one of my mother's expensive silk hand towels. On one particular occasion, we gathered at the edge of a small dirt fissure near the back fence to gave everyone an opportunity to share stories about Jay, the recently deceased kangaroo rat.

"He was a friend to every kid," someone said. We used kite string to unevenly lower the cardboard shoebox into the dirt—the way my brother had seen Churchill slowly interred on television during his state funeral.

And here I was, at 53, moved into adolescent depression by my cat's prognosis. In my slow shuffle across the sweeping steppe of middle age, I have come to accept that life is indeed terminal but also to understand, as Lincoln mused, that "it is not the years of living but the living within the years" that counts. In time, a man may become the things he once ridiculed. As a young invincible, I routinely cast stones at death the way children might throw rocks at headstones as they pass the graveyard.

This milestone was inevitable. Yet I felt unprepared. Death, the thief, was scratching at my window wanting to steal my precious whiskered talisman. In a life so jammed with preconditions and contingencies, I increasingly found delight in the simplest things—my favorite chair, my routine, and the unconditional love I would receive from an ordinary white house cat.

In her youth, Miss Crystal expressed her unconditional love for us in macabre and graphic ways, often leaving what appeared to be a small lima bean or earthworm in a conspicuous location. Upon closer examination, the odd gifts were confirmed to be the internal organs of some unfortunate rodent who could not be identified even by its dental records. Perhaps the bequest was a spleen or a segment of intestine. She radiated feline conceit and like the Victorian madman from east London, could perform complex surgery with a single talon.

On the lethal day she arrived in a crate from JFK, rumors and raw fear circulated through the New Canaan rodent community of a new and terrifying Ripper, an alabaster Lizzy Borden who swept in like a silent avalanche capable of devouring rabbits and small dogs.

She was in fact, a Cinderella story of sorts—a Father Christmas surprise for an eight-year-old girl who was homesick for friends after moving halfway around the world to start a new life with her family.

In the thick of a foggy, cold winter, no animal in England gives birth. Unfazed by the odds of finding a furry companion for my daughter, I contacted every cattery, vet, animal shelter, and pet shop within a 300-mile radius to no avail. The best I could turn up was a black ferret and, of course, rabbits. Miraculously, one store, Pets International Ltd. in southwest London, yielded a possible lead. The owner was somewhat coy and wanted me to come in person.

My visions of a massive pet store filled with grinning kittens and puppies of every possible pedigree yielded to the hard reality of urban London as I passed Ladbroke's off-track betting shops and abandoned buildings interrupted by the occasional Pig and Whistle pub. I warily parked near the shop and entered the Twilight Zone.

"Ahlooow, guv'nuh" the Cockney storeowner bellowed. "Ron, git the white kit from the back, lad, will ya?" A hunched albino teenager with poor teeth shuffled into a maze of cages. That was when the smell hit me like a wave of mustard gas. It was as if I had dived into a colossal dirty diaper that had been buried for weeks just beneath an inch of wood-shavings.

"Yur a lucky one, you are, guv'nuh. Had a geezer in 'ere yesterday that wanted to pay me two 'undred quid for 'er." The boy brought out a filthy white kitten with watering eyes, a bloated stomach, and a persistent sneeze.

"Well, guv'nuh, that'll be 180 quid."

"One-eighty sterling?" I shrieked. "It's just an ordinary house cat."

He sized me up and shook his head, feigning sympathy. "I seems to recall you sayin' you wanted 'er for yer li'l girl."

It's hard to think when you are looking down the gun of a modern-day highwayman, but I called the vet and described the cat's symptoms. The vet was classically British and very non-committal. "Well, Mister Turpin," he said, "I suppose you can wait until spring and find a healthier animal, or you can rescue this poor creature."

This was not the way it was supposed to go. This purchase was supposed to be a sort of Charles Dickens day at an animal Curiosity Shoppe owned by a Fezziwig character who had this amazing kitten with an IQ of an Oxford grad and who smelled like warm chestnuts and Christmas. Fezziwig and I would drink hot rum and laugh about old times we'd never shared. He was supposed to give me the cat for free if I promised I would tithe to the poor.

"Okay, I'll take her," I said.

When I arrived home, I honked for my wife as a signal. With the kids temporarily distracted, we ushered the kitten up to our bathroom and bathed her. As dark, dirty water swirled down the tub, a fluffy snowflake with crystal blue eyes emerged, sneezed, and then padded quietly over to the litter box. She purred loudly as she returned to my wife's lap.

For two long days, we dodged the children's curious questions about our now off-limits bedroom. When Christmas Eve arrived, the plan was to put the cat into a basket and have Brooke find her gift from Father Christmas the next morning. The cat would not cooperate. Terrified of small, enclosed spaces, she would fly at me with fur and claws and frantically tear around the house.

All night I tracked and captured the animal. About six o' clock in the dark dawn of a cold Christmas morning, both cat and man were exhausted, and I succeeded in corralling her long enough to place her in the basket. Brooke came down the stairs and screamed with glee. "He brought her, he brought her! How does Father Christmas do it?"

Looking into the cat's face, she said, "I think I will call her 'Crystal' because she has such blue eyes." I sat exhausted, mindlessly scratching an itch on my arm. It turned out to be ringworm, courtesy of our new family member. In time, we would endear ourselves to many families in SW19 as our cat became the local distributor for the loathsome condition.

Both cat and young girl eventually grew into women but they never stopped cuddling or consoling one across four thousand nights of adolescence. Nighttime would find them in deep conversation, a unilateral discussion about what to wear to school or perhaps whom to invite to tea. She would visit me at night after the children had gone to bed, weaving between my legs like a pilot fish before leaping onto my desk and sitting on my paperwork, daring me to play by knocking every pen, pencil, or moveable object off my desk. She would swat at my hand without baring her claws, boxing and trying to lure me into a game of cat and crab.

She was like Wordsworth's solitary cloud. Her purring reassured us, soothing our trauma in the months following 9-11. She padded her way through fifty-two seasons of life. She always seemed to sense when a gray cloud was crouching on one of our heads and would find us, coaxing us back into her world of gardens and butterflies.

Her foreign policy was fickle: a shrewd mixture of passive-aggression and affection. It soon became apparent that she preferred women to men and children to adults. She would occasionally use her bodily functions as a method of conveying her judgment of people, places, and things. A male house sitter vowed never to return when a simple "present" was left in the middle of his bed. It seemed to suggest that he spend the remaining evenings at his apartment.

Like most pets, she taught us responsibility, the risks and rewards of unconditional love, the vagaries of living with domesticated animals, and the simplicity of sitting in a window watching as the world swirled all around you.

With our adoption of an Australian shepherd pup, the English matron chose voluntary exile upstairs. She loathed the dog and never forgave the gods for upsetting her perfect only-child world. She lived with the girl, watching her grow into a woman, all the while weaving between prom dresses, suitcases, and increasingly long absences. In fits of loneliness, she turned to the inferior boys and on rare occasions would work her way down the stairs to yowl like an alley cat for attention. She resorted to exploring the house in the dead of night—an ancient Grace Poole exploring her former domain, ever wary of the jingling collar of her nemesis, the dog. She had gone from making history to being a relic of a waning age of innocence. Yet she rested and waited for the girl to return, always appreciative of any affection and the attention that came when the upstairs would once again be crowded like a Pullman sleeping car.

I shift off my stiff right shoulder. It's now dark outside and the room is dimly lit. I sit on the floor, my arms stretched under the bed where she rests in the dark, her sides scalping under her ribs as she wrestles with lungs that cannot purge the fluid that keeps filling them. The reassuring purr rises each time I move my hand across her head and down her back. Her tail twitches with a slow, rhythmic snap, a sign of happy fatigue. I scuttle my fingers across the floor emulating a crab. She half-heartedly swats at me and closes her eyes. The greying man and the snow-white grand dame now resting side by side. She moves closer and I touch my nose to hers, prompting her to lick her lips—a kiss goodbye. She falls into a fitful sleep and I descend the stairs.

In the week ahead I would accompany my favorite girl to the vet where we would share one final farewell. She fought hard against the malignancy that slowly invaded her body. When she finally released this life, I watched her spirit rise and float away like a singular snowflake.

Perhaps she will be reincarnated into a magnificent monarch butterfly or a tempestuous French actress. One thing is for certain: Miss Crystal makes my weird little world a better place and left only love—and small rodent spleens— in her wake.

Living in a Fantasy World

> "I like nonsense; it wakes up the brain cells. Fantasy is a necessary ingredient in living, it's a way of looking at life through the wrong end of a telescope. Which is what I do, and that enables you to laugh at life's realities."
> —DR. SEUSS

THE CELL PHONE vibrated against my leg as I sat watching ushers move down the center aisle of the sanctuary carrying plates for tithes and offerings. It was communion Sunday—a service that often had a life of its own, slipping past the expected time of dismissal. I was restless as I saw the LED light flashing through my thin wool slacks. If I could just glance at the...

A "don't even think about it" Puritan laser penetrated my temple as I shifted ever-so-slightly away from my disapproving spouse to see if I could work my phone up to the top of my pocket. I was in the last seat of the aisle with a perfect defilade from everyone except my partner, who was determined to save me from damnation—and from winning my game this week.

I had traveled all week and been unable to complete my Fantasy Football roster. I was waiting for text updates on certain injured players, attempting to gain any insights from the NFL hot stove of experts who would recommend a starter. One of my running backs had suffered a concussion the previous week, and I was desperate to find out if he had passed his cognitive readiness tests. I was undecided between two receivers and trying to find out if a certain All-Pro corner would be returning from injured reserve to defend one of my two wide-outs. Earlier in the week I had begun following two of my players on Twitter hoping I might decipher their castrated missives to divine whether they were going to start.

It is called Fantasy Football because those who play it live in a parallel reality. At times, I prefer this reality to my real one. To enable my addiction, the NFL launched Red Zone, a single station airing only seven hours a week on Sundays and dedicated to tracking every score across fourteen games. On any given Sunday, a total of sixty touchdowns might be faithfully recorded and shared with viewers, while a masthead of Fantasy Football statistics by position and player streams live across the base of one's television. Just thinking about it makes me shiver with delight.

Each week, my fellow owners and I drown ourselves in statistical minutiae, seeking any advantage the way a stock analyst might rummage through the footnotes of a 10-Q filing. If a player is a rookie, we want to know how fast he completed the three-cone drill during the combine. What was his vertical leap? How fast did he run the twenty-yard shuttle?

Part of the FFL addiction is bragging rights. In a time of political correctness, we are less courageous at home or at the office and less inclined to dish insults or speak our minds. Men need outlets. Each week, I look forward to abusing my fellow owners for their missteps that may lead them to start an injured player or not understand the historical significance of how travel and time zones affect West Coast teams that travel east.

When a fellow owner's player is arrested in a pink ballerina outfit, driving the wrong way on an interstate in a car loaded with cans of Red Bull stolen from a Green Bay convenience store, it compels me to write my fellow owner a note of condolence. I'm sure he is feeling disappointed in his player and, like a parent, only wants what's best for his 22-year-old wide receiver making twenty million dollars. The fact that the player brought to the NFL a rap sheet longer than Eminem's and was acquitted for manslaughter while in preschool is of no concern. Can he score touchdowns?

A recent *New York Times* op-ed by C.D. Carter complained that fantasy leagues dehumanize players, essentially turning them into cattle to be bought and sold without regard for them as people. The author was deeply concerned. "Instead of a young running back on the verge of a contract that would mean financial security for his family, we see glistening yards per carry. Instead of an aging quarterback making one last run at glory, we see completion percentages and red zone efficiency."

Well, yeah. I think he just summed up the entire universe of real franchise owners. If you think my lens is a tad jaundiced, try looking at players through the eyes of the media, owners hungry for a return on multimillion-dollar contracts, and coaches whose livelihoods depend on dehumanizing factoids such as completion percentages on third downs, yards after catch, and a young man's probability to avoid arrest for making sexual advances toward beer cart-girls at off-season golf tournaments. Alas, there is no room for delicate sensibilities in either the real or imagined NFL. It's brutal, degrading, and dehumanizing—and then there is the bad side.

I realize some fantasy leagues can get out of hand. One could argue the credit default market was essentially an unregulated financial fantasy league where buyers and sellers were promising to indemnify one another based on whether a third-party debt holder paid or defaulted on loans. That particular league turned out to have no commissioner and be all too real, ending with taxpayers, Lehman Brothers, and the stock market taking a helmet-to-helmet hit.

Other fantasy leagues can get downright bizarre. Consider About2Croak.com, the too-close-for-comfort fantasy league where you get points if your celebrity dies during that particular year. You pick twenty-five celebrities and get points based on a system that subtracts the dead celeb's age from 150. Obviously, your portfolio must include a few sure bets like Betty White, but you get more points if a dark-horse celeb like Miley Cyrus or Lindsay Lohan chooses to steer her Bentley into a telephone pole. Yes, it's sick but hey, that's why I like it. It's schadenfreude on steroids. It's not enough to revel in other's misfortune or death; you want to profit by it. Isn't that what the insurance industry is for?

Sometimes you need to retreat into a world of fantasy. If medicating your difficult day with M&Ms and Manhattans does not move the needle, you may want to disappear into a parallel universe where you can manage a stable of warriors and win fame with shrewd trades and cunning insights. You can be king or queen for a day and the master and commander of your private cabal of friends. In my case, it's an eight-man breakfast club that convenes most weekends to commiserate and compare notes on life, sports, and trends that make life worth living, such as friends and Fantasy Football.

So I'm back in church and I am still distracted. Who should I start, Andre Johnson or Josh Gordon? Maybe I'll sit Gordon and put in Chris Ivory as my flex player. What to do? I need a burning bush. Actually, I wish I had *Reggie* Bush, but someone else got him.

My minister reads a piece on world mission and discusses the riches of ancient times. Gold, silver, ivory...

Did he say ivory?

It's a sign. I reach for my phone to add Chris Ivory of the Jets.

My wife frowns and whispers, "Put that away, right now."

"I have to submit my line."

She has a black belt in emasculating looks of disapproval. I roll my eyes and abandon the phone. I know better than to take on my commissioner.

After the service, our minister greets us. Knowing his passion for the Chicago Bears and keeping in mind the memory of my wife's lingering disdain, I confessed my act of spiritual insubordination. He smiled and leaned in, "Go with Josh Gordon. Schaub is playing terrible and can't throw the ball to Johnson. Besides Cleveland is up against Atlanta and they rank last against the pass. Both corners are injured."

I pursed my lips and raised my eyebrows in approval. I knew I liked this guy. As I walked out to the Common Room, I heard him call behind me.

"But remember, God is a Bears fan."

The Mythology of Us

*"I believe that imagination is stronger than knowledge—myth
is more potent than history—dreams are more powerful
than facts—hope always triumphs over experience—
laughter is the cure for grief—love is stronger than death."*
—ROBERT FULGHUM

I N FARLEY MOWAT'S *Never Cry Wolf*, a young wildlife biologist named
Tyler is dispatched by the Canadian Wildlife Service to investigate whether the Arctic wolf is to blame for the decline of the great caribou herds in
the Alaskan wilderness. Tyler's adventure is a life-altering journey through the
looking glass where every preconceived notion of survival is cast aside by the
harsh cunning of the wild.

With the help of some local Inuit, the young biologist becomes one with
the savage landscape and in doing so, he discovers that the Arctic wolf, *Canus
lupus arctos*, is not the indiscriminate killer of caribou but, in fact, is culling the
herds of their sicker and weaker members, all but ensuring the herds' survival.
In the vast emptiness of an Arctic twilight during which the summer breathes
but a few endless nights of day, Tyler discovers the power of Inuit mythology.

As the acrid smoke of a burning fire creates broken shafts of light inside
the makeshift Inuit shelter, a tribal elder recounts to some younger members
of his tribe how the wolf came into existence. In the form of native myth, the

ancient sage, Ootek, shares with Tyler and the Inuit children how Mother Earth first created the People and then realized she must provide food to sustain them. In her infinite wisdom, she reached into an ebony hole in the ice and pulled out the tuktu (caribou) to feed them.

"Soon the tuktu had multiplied to such a level that food became scarce and overpopulation created a generation of sick and weak animals. Their decline threatened the very existence of the People. The great Mother once again reached into the black hole of ice and pulled out the amarok (Arctic wolf) to whom the task fell to thin the overpopulated herds of the sick and weak thus ensuring a stronger generation so that the People might thrive."

Ootek smiles a toothless grin and nods his head. Tyler watches these lessons being handed down—worn gifts of insight wrapped in a timeless skin of mythology. At that moment, he eases backwards, arms folded behind his head, pondering the brightest stars as they struggle through a permanent summer twilight. Beams of smoke and light escape from a thousand seams between the roof of broken pine boughs and caribou antlers. Tyler finally comes to understand through Ootek's ancient mythology that Arctic wilderness is a last Garden of Eden, ingeniously balanced with each supporting actor playing a vital role in the symbiotic dance for survival. Everything is here for a reason.

In the end, Ootek, the old one, comes to accept Tyler as one of his own, teaching him the mythology and traditions that serve as guideposts for survival. In Inuit society, as in the life of the wolf pack, there is no such thing as an orphan.

As the campfires of our own summers dwindle to tangerine glows, we may reflect on the time we spend trying to recapture the power of simple things—a gathering of our own tribe and perhaps the retelling of our own stories. For many, the memory of youthful stories and early American mythology has been erased. We have lost our all-powerful talismans—a rabbit's foot, a shark's tooth, or a ten-banded Diamondback's rattle. Myths are no longer handed down and perpetuated.

As a society, we no longer wonder how we came to be and instead focus on what is yet to come. Faith and wonder have been supplanted by anxious impatience for instant resolution. In taming and deconstructing the natural world, we have marginalized the virtues of mythology as a way of understanding how we fit into the endless continuum of humanity.

Today's tribal family no longer lives among multiple generations. Our children do not enjoy as much access to or have the patience to rest at the feet of an elderly relative who is eager to paint a picture with the sepia tones of the past. With so much "reality" barraging us every day, there is no room left for myth.

We have moved up Maslow's hierarchy—migrating from the basic needs for shelter, immediate family, and the stories that served as framework for living—to a more permanent and material state of perpetual want. Many families no longer dine together, spend time in the same room, or express curiosity about their own unique history. The "snobbery of chronology," as C.S. Lewis called it, is believing we are superior to all that came before us because we have the benefit of hindsight. As a society, we seem to be moving away from our own mythology of self-reliance, sacrifice, generosity, naive optimism, and independence to a place where we are more cynically defined by what we own.

Writer Umberto Eco once mused, "In the United States there's a Puritan ethic and a mythology of success. He who is successful is good. In Latin countries and in Catholic countries, a successful person is a sinner." Eco's European view is born from a very different life experience and a complex notion of how values, wants, needs, desires, and expectations are reconciled when man by definition is meant to suffer to achieve wisdom and humility.

Americans are a mass of contradictions. We are modern families—fractured and yet still hanging together by the threads of our own potential. But many of us have forgotten our own narratives.

I look for occasions to impart these stories to my children. As they grow older, they consider their own heritage and the mythology of their ancestors to be trite and dated fables that serve little purpose. Yet on the right evening I can still entice them with a wartime story of their British great-grandfather digging victims of a V-1 rocket attack out of a bomb shelter in London or a distant ancestor whose Ohio home was part of the miraculous and dangerous Underground Railroad.

They have learned of a mongrel heritage of confederates, saints, villains, nobility, and cutthroats. Our personal mythology rises out of tragedy and often chronicles individuals who had the misfortune of being born in a time when they were overwhelmed by circumstances. They were first-generation Irish, German, French, and English immigrants. They were soldiers killed fighting for the English army with General Kitchener at Omdurman. Some died of fever and others endured physical and mental hardships. A famous uncle was the only cavalry officer killed as he rode with Jeb Stuart around the flanks of the egotistical Union general George McClellan. A painting depicting the "Tragic Death of Lt. William Latané, C.S.A," hangs in capitol in Richmond, Virginia.

The kids quiet down as I paint a canvas of a restless Irishman wearing Union indigo, clutching his glistening bayonet and staring across a frozen December battlefield at Fredericksburg. There was also a Chicago inventor and entrepreneur: Dan Canary. He ran a taxi service recognized for its unique canary-yellow cabs.

Years later, he would protest that John Hertz had stolen his idea of the Canary cab by launching the iconic Yellow Cab Manufacturing Company. Dan never won his case against Hertz, and in the process he lost his first wife, leaving him a widower with eight children. Ever the resourceful man, he married a considerably younger woman he met through a mail-order bride firm. They had three more girls, one of whom was my grandmother, Ruth Farr Canary.

Whether we were once Huguenots escaping religious persecution or indentured souls willing to risk everything for a new start, our families have evolved from the DNA of stronger ancestors who endured, suffered, refused to acquiesce, and searched the horizon-line for a better way forward.

These fireside moments are the times I cherish as I harvest history and leaven in wholesome doses of our own mythology—a bloated narrative of how my father walked miles to school through snow in urban Chicago or how a mischievous uncle swam in a Florida alligator pond on a drunken dare. I work these stories into an endless book of virtues in hopes that these seeds might one day germinate at a time of crisis or decision.

When I think of the attributes I want my children to exhibit when they finally are released into the unforgiving wilderness of man, I wonder what I have done this week, this month, or this year to plant those seeds of character and virtue, generously fertilizing the life lessons with myths, stories, and the history of us.

Our personal and American mythology is a wonderful tale of survival, noble deeds, redemption, human frailty, and the progression from self to selfless. Like the Inuit fables, these stories remind us of our potential as individuals and as a nation. Our greatness has not been completely stripped, overdrawn, sold, stolen, or spent. It is here, waiting to be rediscovered in new places: to be excavated, mined, and processed into the virtues of patience, hard work, and the courage to change.

Perhaps the mountain that looms ahead won't seem so steep if our children come to understand the legends and folklore of those who climbed before them. Whether it is coming to see our natural world as a living, breathing entity or realizing that the impossible is a self-imposed limitation, our mythology can teach an entire generation to reverse our self-destructive course and speak up over the voices of the false prophets and political charlatans.

We need our mythology to survive. Robert Redford recently warned a small audience that time is running out. "I believe in mythology," he said. "I guess I share Joseph Campbell's notion that a culture or society without mythology will eventually disappear, and some might argue we're close to that already."

It seems as if we have left something behind. In our single-mindedness to succeed and overcome the very obstacles that helped define us and make us stronger, we have abandoned our past. We must rise again and reclaim the best parts of ourselves. And like puzzles, we fill in our own missing pieces one at a time—through a communal story, a shared value or, collective belief. These are the anchors that underpin us and allow society to believe that in time, we can become a better version of ourselves.

The Return of François Egalité

*"We love our superheroes because they refuse to give up
on us. We can analyze them out of existence, kill them, ban
them, mock them, and still they return, patiently reminding
us of who we are and what we wish we could be."*

—GRANT MORRISON

A S A KID, I had an overactive imagination and a short attention span. I was chastised as a "daisy gazer" by baseball coaches and as "lacking social responsibility" by my spinster teacher, Miss Austin, whose last boyfriend was in the Polk administration. With regularity, I was marched off to see the principal, Miss Pratt, for infractions ranging from insubordination and inattentiveness to telling whopping half-truths such as my father was an operative for the CIA. He was, after all, in advertising, which involved propaganda and the subliminal manipulation of the masses. I was certain he was writing pro bono vignettes for Radio Free Europe on the side.

I was a junior version of James Thurber's Walter Mitty, fantasizing and daydreaming my time away. I was the short man dreaming of slam-dunking a basketball or the flat-footed Clydesdale gazing into the mud puddle and wishing he were Man O' War. I invented alter egos and super heroes. I lived their lives vicariously until my mind and body stretched to afford me my own adventures. However, I never stopped filling in the cracks and dimly lit spaces of my prosaic routine with dashing figures and adventurers. Over time, life carved its hard lines on my face. My idealistic penchant for undisputed resolution and redemption rusted under the constant corrosive exposure to society's moral ambiguity and materialism. My imagination faltered and my adolescent propensity to dream was lost like an old blanket or stuffed toy.

Years later, I find myself once again seeking to escape from a slate-gray world where people play by different sets of rules, bad deeds go unpunished, and the guy with the most expensive attorney gets off. I long for a black-and-white corner of the universe where there are distinguishable good and bad guys who wear different color uniforms and work for agencies with names like "Control" and "Chaos." We need a hero who rides a white horse and is just a second faster on the draw and a system where bad guys always get nailed as they are boarding their United flight to Buenos Aires with the employee pension funds.

I find myself once again conjuring up an imaginary protagonist: François Egalité, a master businessman and international man of intrigue. He is Louis Jourdan, Hercule Poirot and James Bond rolled into one. The French have flair and Egalité is no exception. He races cars in Monaco, seduces starlets such as Audrey Tautou and Sophie Marceau, and wears a signature silk cravat.

Egalité is the perfect cover name for a hero who saves governments, captures evil industrialists, and is able to spell "vichyssoise." Egalité has contempt for inequity, as it is the antithesis of his surname. He is a champion of the exploited, the underrepresented, and the sartorially challenged. After saving yet another magnificent buxom heiress from the harem of a petro-authoritarian sheik or protecting a French farmer with twelve children from losing his land to a corrupt agricultural monopoly, Egalité always melts into the cool shadows, leaving a calling card with his trademark fleur de lis insignia and the rearranged French national motto: "Liberté, Fraternité...and Egalité!" We need François Egalité to come out of retirement from his hillside chateau in Biarritz, where he paints plein air ocean scenes and lives with his Serbian scientist girlfriend Chloe and his Samoyed husky Ça Va.

In the world of Egalité, guys who bilk investors of fifty billion dollars don't sit at home under house arrest watching Rachael Ray make Mexican flan. They are kidnapped under the nose of the Feds, fitted with cement tennis shoes, and asked where all the loot is stashed. Once the information is extracted, Egalité challenges the evil Ponzi schemer to recover a euro that Egalité has tossed into the East River. Egalité is last seen leaning over the bridge, yelling at a dissolving swirl of bubbles with his hand to his ear, "Pardon, Mssr. Ponzi? What is it you say? You cannot swing? Oh, you said swim?"

I conjure up Egalité as I read another depressing headline. The Metro North jolts noisily across the Harlem River into a restless city of insomniacs and shattered financiers. New York seems a giant restless leg, twitching and tapping while furtively looking for signs and signals as to what clouds might be next on the horizon. I walk up Park Avenue, another cardboard cutout wearing a London Fog overcoat and lugging an ancient, scuffed Tumi handbag. Steam rises out of grates as workmen wrapped in odd mummy-like mufflers bark at one another through great plumes of frozen air.

My mind drifts. And I am once again François Egalité, corporate whistle blower and a member of the Free Market League of Consumer Advocates. Like Kwai Chang Caine, from the old TV show *Kung Fu*, I am a restless wanderer, moving from company to company, trying to escape my past but inevitably drawn into a web of corruption and malfeasance. With each new position, I think this time it will be different, only to have the dog dirt hit the fan. One week, I discover the nice HR manager with whom I share a lunch bench each day is secretly skimming cash by using child laborers in Romania. Next month, it is a megalomaniacal CEO who is timing his stock options. Next month, it could be a CFO whose cooked books rival The Barefoot Contessa's.

The revelations usually come to me from a frightened middle manager as we graze on leftover C-Suite sandwiches abandoned like soup kitchen hand-outs in our microscopic lunchroom. My new friend is from accounting and confides her concern over the strike price of the CEO's options. I get that old sinking feeling that a Pandora's Box is about to be opened. It is my curse and my raison d'être: to root out corruption. I smile as I think about the time Egalité tied the hands of a corrupt inside-trading controller with his own Hermès tie. How ironic!

In the end, Egalité protects the little guy but always has to move on—a tragic corporate drifter like *The Fugitive*'s Richard Kimball or *The Incredible Hulk*'s Dr. David Banner. In Egalité's case, he is not so much running from anything but instead just trying to clean up American business so he might return to Chloe and Ça Va.

It is time for Egalité to come back to America. There are white-collar criminals to catch, forensic accounting to find hidden Swiss bank accounts, and jobs to save.

A taxi honks at me and I jolt to reality as I loiter in the street. I look up to realize I have walked past my office by twelve blocks. I am standing in front of an Hermès store.

Mon Dieu, this must be a sign.

We're Still Together

"My advice to you is to get married. If you find a good wife,
you'll be happy; if not, you'll become a philosopher."
—SOCRATES

I N A BASKETBALL coaching career that may never be equaled, John Wooden won a remarkable 664 games and lost a mere 162. His UCLA teams won 10 national championships in 12 years, including seven in a row from 1966 to1973. During this period, his teams won 88 straight games. Throughout his career, he led four different teams to perfect 30-0 seasons.

If you were to have asked John Wooden about the greatest decision in his remarkable career, he would unquestionably point to his decision to marry Nellie Riley, his high school sweetheart, in 1932. Nellie was the center of John's universe and the person he claimed knew him better than he knew himself. He once remarked that marriage, like sports, did not build character but revealed it.

Nellie and John were married for fifty-three years before she died of cancer in 1985. Before he passed in 2010, John Wooden would mark the calendar for the 21st of each month and pen a love letter to Nell, his best friend. Sports journalist Rick Reilly reports that at Wooden's death more than 260 letters were stacked neatly on her pillow, tied with a yellow ribbon. Nellie's side of the bed they shared remained undisturbed. When asked by Reilly if he was afraid to die, the then 90-year-old Wooden remarked, "Of course not. Death is my only chance to be with her again."

With more than one of every two American marriages ending in divorce, its even odds at best for couples to make it to the mountaintop together. British author Len Deighton once wrote, "The tragedy of marriage is that while all women marry thinking that their man will change, all men marry believing their wife will never change."

In any relationship each of us is really three people—the person we project to the world, the person we secretly see ourselves to be, and the person our partner knows. It's that last person who is probably the most accurate version of who we really are. Most relationships get into trouble when the chasm between our face to the world and the person our partner knows becomes too great. It seems the more we seek to be the same person all the time, the more capacity we have to focus on others, which is the essential ingredient to love and the antithesis of self-worship.

It is a paradox of the human condition that we seem to gravitate toward our opposites. My theory is that every relationship includes an agitator and a fixer. The agitator is the expressive, aggressive, and more mercurial partner, while the fixer is the moderating influence, the rock, and a steady hand. When two agitators marry, the combination can be combustible. When two fixers exchange vows, the relationship may seem the equivalent to watching paint dry. Yet while our personal styles bring a rich trousseau to the marriage, the foundations that remain the strongest are those built on shared values. When we see one another for who we are and who we are not, forgiving our limitations and reveling in our possibilities, a relationship breaks out of its chrysalis and takes wing.

In the land of the blind, the one-eyed man is king, and in love it is our ability to reflect, even momentarily, that sometimes prevents us from falling prey to the cotton candy rush of immediate physical attraction. We all learn the hard way that the currents of a relationship change with the trade winds of time: the arrival of children; life events that challenge our faith in one another;

illness; success; disappointment; and death. Woody Allen mused that a relationship "is like a shark. It has to keep moving forward or it dies."

Those who have been married for decades do not gild the lily of love. They talk of constant compromise, trying to avoid taking one another for granted, expressing appreciation, offering forgiveness, making time, playing the mood music, seeking to understand before seeking to be understood, recognizing perfect moments, never forgetting that anything you put ahead of each other eventually comes between you, and remembering that resentment is liking drinking poison and waiting for the other person to die. As these couples hurtle through life and fall prey to life's ruts and distractions, they always circle back to find one another. "A marriage," Honoré de Balzac said, "must constantly fight the monster which devours everything: routine."

Commitment is not 50/50 but in fact two people giving 100 percent. When the rate of change outside the relationship exceeds the rate of change within it, the end is near. Many endure dark passages where they are overwhelmed by excessive responsibility or self-pity and must fight the instinct to abandon ship. Some idealize relationships and love, wondering why their best-laid plans are constantly sabotaged. Others make the mistake of comparing their private insides to other people's public veneers. We cannot resist the invitation when *Cosmopolitan* asks us to "rate our mate." We forget that Oscar Wilde assured us that "the only normal people you know are the people you do not know very well."

And we are still together. A gentle sigh in the dark of midnight. A smile across a crowded room. An extemporaneous moment at a piano recital that is memorable only because it was shared. Flash points, disagreements, and tired, lazy shortcuts can lead to hurt feelings, but most of us find our way back to one another like emotional strays that, once fed, keep returning for sustenance. For all their periodic insanity, we need our relationships. Perhaps some of our stories are not as romantic as John and Nellie Wooden's, but we all have chapters remaining to be written. Our experiences together are the fine threads in our common tapestry of commitment. Each couple is its own unique work of art. And the beauty of that art is always in the eyes of the beholder.

The End of the Myth

"A gun is a tool, Marion, no better or no worse than any other tool, an axe, a shovel or anything. A gun is as good or as bad as the man using it. Remember that."
—ALAN LADD IN *SHANE*

MOST OF US have seen a western. The influences of western mythology and its romantic qualities are inexorably bound to American society. The ideals and ethics embodied in the western myth have been celebrated through the film genre. The post-World War II generation spent countless hours in dark theatres immersed in the epic moment of the west—a moment that existed in a time when our virgin continent beckoned settlers to farm its lush valleys and conquer its high mountains. It depicted a time of possibility, when no social or economic impediments could keep good people from realizing their dreams. In this epic moment, the settlers stood face to face with the forces of nature and overcame all obstacles to realize their manifest destiny.

There were clear heroes and villains. Perhaps most memorable was the western hero who was the embodiment of all the virtues in society. Actors such as John Wayne, Jimmy Stewart, Gary Cooper, Randolph Scott, and Alan Ladd became larger-than-life incarnations of all that was true and right in America. In these classic westerns, directors such as John Ford, George Stevens, and Howard Hawks manipulated the myth, creating romantic distractions and a deep longing for simpler times.

George Stevens' *Shane*, set in the pristine yet dramatically menacing Teton Valley, is perhaps the quintessential classic western film. As Shane rides into the frame, he appears like a savior in a saddle, a lone, almost supernatural figure in buckskin descending into a valley to defend honest homesteaders against a corrupt rancher. Befriended by the Starrett family, Shane is seen through the eyes of young Joey Starrett, who idolizes the mysterious visitor. Shane temporarily removes his buckskins and tries to become part of the community. However, at his core, Shane is a gunfighter who cannot shake his violent past. In the end, he straps on his guns and resolves the homesteaders' conflicts, but now, having unleashed his violence, he must once again leave the community for inevitable isolation. As Shane rides away from the valley, young Joey Starrett is heard yelling, "Shane, come back!"

Not unlike Shane, the classic western soon found itself unable to live among a changing society. Film is reflexive. It serves as a mirror of our communities and points of view. As the '50s became the '60s, new westerns emerged—films that questioned the myth and in some ways implied that the myth was corrupt. Directors began to view the taming of the west as a time when settlers contaminated a New World Garden of Eden. The men and women that had been depicted as blameless, endearing, strong, and brave were transformed into ambiguous characters who sullied the very land they possessed. The new western offered less romantic, grittier realism and heroes who were morally and personally paradoxical.

John Ford was perhaps the most successful of all classic western directors. His films—*Stagecoach*, *The Three Godfathers*, *Fort Apache*, and *My Darling Clementine*—all set among the red rock cathedrals of Monument Valley, depicted a west as wild as the dust devils and chaparral winds that buffeted the crude homesteads and forts at the edge of civilization. After WWII, Ford returned with a darker vision of the west in *The Searchers* and *The Man Who Shot Liberty Valence*. New directors Martin Ritt, Arthur Penn, Robert Altman, and Sam Peckinpah painted a west where blood and violence—all signature symptoms of encroaching civilization—were brought to the Garden in the name of progress. In the end, our aspiration to tame Eden revealed deep fissures in our character and, like missionaries, we unintentionally polluted the land and people we sought to tame.

McCabe and Mrs. Miller, Little Big Man, Lonely Are the Brave, Will Penny, and *The Wild Bunch* represented a new genre of film: the contemporary western. In Penn's *Little Big Man,* Native Americans were referred to as The People and the film's revisionist and satirical deconstruction of the epic moment left us with a bitter taste for the epic west.

In these movies, sinners were as responsible as saints for the founding of western society. Heroes died, cheated in fights, shot people in the back, swore, slept with prostitutes, and often made the wrong decisions. Like all of us, they were flawed. The flawed protagonist dovetailed with our pessimistic view of society and echoed a deep longing for a mythic west that perhaps never existed except in the minds of dime novelists and on the canvases of the great Western artists: Albert Bierstadt, Thomas Moran, Charles Russell, and Frederic Remington.

In the '70s, we returned to the epic moment, but it was no longer in the west. It was in outer space. *Star Wars* recreated the epic moment of good and evil clashing in a virgin wonderland where anything was possible. Siths and Jedis were the gunfighters, but the western epic moment was gone. A few modern-day westerns briefly caught our imaginations, but as Lawrence Kasden, director of *Silverado,* noted, "Nearly every western over the last ten years has failed, except for *Dances with Wolves.*"

America needs westerns now more than ever. We need to be reminded of a time when heroes were celebrated and heroism took many shapes: the courage to reinvent oneself, stand up for what was right, fight corrupting influences, and live a life defined by a firm set of morals and beliefs.

Maybe the epic moment of the west really never existed, but it appeals so deeply to us because each of us secretly longs for a more innocent time. Why is it, then, that the western film is no longer commercially viable? Perhaps we have gotten to the point where our own cynicism precludes us from believing in all its possibilities. Or perhaps even worse, we can no longer even recognize them when we see them.

Brotherhood and the Dead

"Music is an outburst of the soul."
—FREDERICK DELIUS

AS A CHILD of the '60s and'70s, I used music and lyrics as a primitive Rosetta Stone to decipher a confusing world of mixed messages about love, social responsibility, and any form of authority. As a third child, I benefited from and at times paid a price for emulating my older brothers. My siblings were accidental role models whose every word and action would be registered and filed in my mental folder of what could be defined as "cool." Their clothes, hobbies, habits, and especially their music were all fair game to be plagiarized, borrowed, or stolen to fill the white canvas of my own vanilla existence.

At night I listened to songs that concussed through my older brothers' bedroom doors. Downstairs, in my father's den, he grimaced at the rattling light fixture, enduring a ten-minute instrumental jam like an artillery barrage from massive JBL and Bose speakers.

"Turn that shit down!"

But like the proverbial problem tenant in any upstairs apartment, the music never stayed down for long. I would tap my pencil on the living room table to the electric riffs of Carlos Santana; the whimsical a capella of Crosby, Stills, Nash & Young; the bellicose sounds of Jim Morrison; the smooth midnight sax of John Klemmer; the precision of Eric Clapton; the sweet sounds of Joni Mitchell; the dulcet blue grass of Poco; the confederate militancy of the Allman Brothers; the twisted, dirty love of Frank Zappa; and a dozen other long-haired iconoclasts. Their harmonies were a revelation and each song plunged me through the looking glass, urging me to shed the conventions of my risk-averse, soft suburban life.

As kids, we spent hours listening to music. It was the centerpiece to any gathering and the accompaniment to every significant personal milestone—the first girlfriend, the break-up, the epic eight-keg party that got us grounded until 2089, or the freshman year week spent at Camp Fox on Santa Catalina Island. When combined with the raw emotion of adolescence, music left an indelible mark and would forever allow us to instantly relive any moment when the initial chords of a particular song flickered to life. If our tastes took us toward rock or easy listening, we might find ourselves quoting Jackson Browne or Kenny Loggins. If we were edgy and unsettled, we would search for musicians who gave words and sound to emotions that were struggling to swim to the surface of our own inarticulate existence. At 13, we were too young to know The Man, but we were sure he and all his other controlling, authoritarian friends were working overtime to keep us down.

Music was an emotional thread that bound us together in a time of social change. To adopt someone's music was tantamount to patching into a gang. With the knowledge divined from hours of listening to artists, I formed a bridge to my brothers and to an older tribe of teens who had seen the Garden, tasted its forbidden fruit, and not spent the rest of the night throwing it up.

Older brothers are an eternal a two-edged sword. On one hand, they tormented me and years later were identified in therapy as the genesis of my body image issues. Twenty years of being called "pumpkin head" can make a guy uncomfortable buying hats or going out on Halloween. Yet my brothers were also a blessing and important lines of sight in the shrouded topography of youth. Big brothers were always one step ahead in the jungle of life—walking point, vanquishing bullies, explaining life in simple terms and, most importantly, breaking in the parents with "firsts"—the first car wreck, the first suspension from school, or the first unsanctioned party. Brothers were family standard bearers who modified the bar of unrealistic expectation.

My eldest brother, Miles, took the most hits. He was my father's first exposure to a world he could not control. A son was a tenured employee who could not be fired for various acts of "grab ass" that would normally invite a pink slip at work. Miles was exposed to the full radiation of our conservative father, who went into parenting believing that he brought us into this world and he had a right to take us out of it. By the time my two older brothers, Miles and Tom, had gone to college, they had domesticated my parents and left my younger brother and me with guardrails that had lost much of their electricity. By 1976, the year of our nation's bicentennial, my parents had initiated the withdrawal of their ground troops, abandoned the embassy, and reluctantly afforded my younger brother and me a level of self-governance. The youngest, Patrick, flourished under this laissez-faire regime, while I took full advantage of the new freedom to find trouble.

I owe my siblings many things. They were human shields unlucky in their birth order but capable of navigating the more punitive reactions of a loving but determined father as he desperately tried to fight the riptides of the sybaritic and psychedelic '60s. Their bedroom walls were plastered with posters of peace signs, pot leaves, surfers, and Dennis Hopper flipping off America from his hog in *Easy Rider*. But the posters were chump change compared to the music. The acid rock and seditious lyrics bugged my dad. It was the clarion call of war—one generation declaring management no longer fit for duty.

One band in particular seemed to offend all conservative, Nixon-loving hard hats. This particular San Francisco troupe captured the essence of the decade's commitment to sex, psychedelic drugs, and rock and roll. Their music and lyrics were Trojan horse socialistic vessels espousing drug use and reckless behavior. Their skeleton-riddled album covers identified them as The Grateful Dead. Most just called them The Dead.

While The Grateful Dead became heroes to a generation who felt the need to find a new community to follow, the band was viewed by anyone in authority as gateway to trouble. Any group with a name like The Dead must be a nihilistic bunch of freeloading potheads who lived like cockroaches in the lava lamplight of the Haight in San Francisco. The neighborhood was a notorious hotbed of acid, promiscuity, and socialism. It might as well have been an annexed suburb of Moscow.

Conservatives shook their heads at this group of druggy miscreants. Their lead singer looked Jewish, had a Hispanic surname, and was missing a finger on one of his hands. He had probably lost his digit helping Huey Newton and the Black Panthers make pipe bombs. The other guitarist looked like a deadbeat with deep-set serial-killer eyes and a hustler's dimpled chin. The band exuded waste and consumption. The more the establishment derided The Dead, the more drawn we were to their melodies.

The Dead sang about life—a hard and entangled existence filled with complicated relationships, drugs, free spirits, lost jobs, and abandoned love. They were the mongrel offspring of blue grass, psychedelic rock, and gritty Southern blues. It seemed axiomatic even in our own house: one man's white trash was another generation's treasure.

Dead concerts were rumored to be a massive electric Kool-Aid acid tests where individuals would alter their brain chemistry in search of a deeper meaning to the music and as an excuse to rotate uncontrollably for hours. The Dead were not just a band; they were a frame of mind and a vibe. The Dead Nation was a series of rippling concentric circles whose core was populated by roadies and traveling Deadheads and whose outer rings comprised posers and people who just wanted to sing the refrain to "Casey Jones."

The actual concerts ranged from strange meandering acoustical journeys to raucous benders. The Dead did not always headline their concerts and shared the marquee with some legendary bands and performers. The combinations were often epic and spontaneous. The core of every concert always swirled around the self-anointed laity of Deadheads—a permanent diaspora of misfits and free spirits who would follow the band as they crisscrossed the country and continents.

As fans, we each had our favorite songs and albums. Like Rob Fleming in Nick Hornsby's *High Fidelity*, we had a Dead song for every occasion and a top ten list for each life moment. A blue circumspect mood might invite "Unbroken

Chain" or "Black Peter," while an afternoon pool party would not be complete without "Sugar Magnolia" and "Eyes of the World." The orthodox Deadheads were more resolute in their obsession. Favorite songs would include dates and venues and invite until-dawn debates about where one might have heard the best rendition of "Bertha" or "Momma Tried."

"No dude, you're wrong. 'Cassidy' at the Orpheum, July 16, 1976. That was Bobby at his best!"

"Nay. I must disagree, my good man. The Dead opening for Chuck Berry at Winterland 1967. Get real! Garcia earns his nickname, Captain Trips."

"Excusé-moi. Three words. Fillmore East 1970. The Dead and the Allman Brothers."

"Bonehead, you were like ten when they played at the Orpheum."

Silence.

"Listen, man, my buddy played me this radical bootleg of the concert. It's all you need to know."

Other merry wanderers would delight in producing barely audible bootleg tapes of concerts or quoting obscure songs written by Hunter and Garcia or Weir and Barlow. A Dead enthusiast might know that the song "Ripple" was as rare as California rain and played a mere thirty-eight times across a 15-year period from the mid-seventies to late eighties.

The goal of every aspiring Deadhead was to work across a dozen weekends to accumulate enough scratch to buy tickets to your first concert. It was where the future was waiting.

Every kid lied about his or her experiences at rock concerts. Pilgrims returned from Dead shows with exaggerated reports of behavior not witnessed since Caligula's Rome. Although their memories seemed to mirror those fanciful tales featured in the *Penthouse Forum*, most came for the music and left on two feet. A few ended up discovering some new boundary, which meant missing most of the concert because they were throwing up in bathroom, frantic because they thought the moon was following them, or were simply worn down from trying to get the phone number of a spinning ballerina named Prairie Flower, a wispy free spirit whose Mendocino commune did not have electricity or an address.

Teens attending their first concert were appropriately wary and at the same time desperate to find excess and perhaps discover some latent aspect of their personality that could be revealed only in the uninhibited cocoon of a Dead show.

We felt a part of an exclusive but accepting tribe. We were not alone. According to the website *Bio*, merry Boomer Deadheads included an odd mixture of liberal and conservative from Bill Walton, Barack Obama, and Steve Jobs to Walter Cronkite, Ann Coulter, and white-collar executives who were desperate to temporarily escape a predictable life. The ultimate sin was to become what Jackson Brown referred to as a "pretender" living in the shade of a freeway.

My first Dead show marked my sixteenth birthday at the Santa Barbara County Bowl. I found myself wandering among a new breed of people who lived outside my suburban bubble. The crowd moved like wildlife across the green-grass infield, spinning and dancing like human dreidels. Inhibition had left the city limits and in its wake was a visceral Summer of Love zeitgeist. The contact high was both symbolic and genuine as the police retreated into a soft, midnight-blue perimeter.

After eight hours of multiple bands and artists headlined by The Dead, we found ourselves separated from our friends and unable to find our ride home to Los Angeles. We navigated two miles to an on-ramp of Highway 101 and hung out our thumbs to hitchhike to an agreed gathering spot. Up to this point I had been afraid even to take a public bus. A beaten Ford coughed to a stop as four Deadheads bound for San Diego and the next Dead show welcomed us into their vehicle. A hundred miles later, we spilled out of the ride and caught a cab the rest of the way home.

Over the years, I would scour the Calendar/Arts section of the LA Times and delight when I saw The Dead coming to any venue within five hundred miles. I would abandon whatever trappings of responsibility I had accumulated to that point and disappear among the hippies and free spirits. There was never any judgment, only great music. I'd return the following Monday with stories and a sense that I had once again pushed the reset button of my life. I was still truckin', looking for familiar faces in a sea of joyous humanity.

Over the years, my obligations overcame my sense of adventure and I found myself becoming a father in every sense of the word. I stopped attending Dead shows, but in times of intense responsibility, found myself wishing I could follow The Dead to Egypt and perhaps climb the Great Pyramids at dawn with Bill Walton and Bob Weir. To follow the band was to live a tumbleweed existence rolling from venue to venue, sleeping on couches and park benches. I have friends who have followed artists. But bands broke apart and best friends self-destructed as a result of egos and hubris. Those other tribes could not replicate the sense of total self-determination that came with the life of a Deadhead.

The band never won a Grammy for an album or a song in the fifty years they performed for millions of fans. They finally were rewarded with a lifetime achievement Grammy but might never find the fickle Rock & Roll Hall of Fame. They represented something deeper to a generation that was told it must choose between a two-party system defined by success or want. Happiness was an outgrowth of one's accomplishment, not an end state. We opted for door number three.

Just as Jeff Bridges' *The Big Lebowski* struck a chord with a generation of Gen Xers who had become cynical about the material finish line they were chasing, The Dead were minstrels for a turbulent time. For Boomers, life's goal of meeting or exceeding some standard of living seemed so in conflict with joy. Happiness was getting what you wanted but it had an expiration date that came all too soon. Joy was measured in minutes of freedom and days spent living in harmony with and for others.

Our job description was to break the shackles of angry, Old Testament patriarchs who viewed dissension as tantamount to social anarchy. The ethos of the music was about love and disappointment, success, failure, and the gritty reality that so many people find as they navigate the shoals of real life—a life that bore no relation to the Brady Bunch. Our time on earth was *Howl's Moving Castle*. It had no permanence except in experience found in other people and other places. Within a single ballad, The Dead's music and lyrics could transform the darkest alley into a calm illuminated fireside.

Thirty-seven years later across a half-lifetime of change, I found The Dead again. A series of farewell concerts would take place over five nights in Palo Alto and Chicago.

On a soft Sunday night, a light San Francisco Bay breeze swept across a tangled sea of gray hair and tie-dyed shirts as a thousand illuminated phones flashed like fireflies in the twilight.

I was a spiritual swallow descending on Levi Stadium, accompanied by two of my kids, my brother Tom, his wife, and a close childhood friend who had opened his home to us in Menlo Park. Each pilgrim, fueled by nostalgia, came for a different reason. Most came just to once again smell the jasmine scents of their own adolescence and gather for a final time to celebrate the music of their lives.

We were suddenly all 18 again (bad backs and all), ready to leap tall buildings with a single bound. On the second night of a three-night set, 75-year-old year old Phil Lesh, the bassist and liver transplant survivor, thanked the audience and rhetorically laughed about their fifty-year run.

"Who would have thought?"

My mind drifted to the distinct vocals and guitar work of their missing leader, Jerry Garcia. Trey Anastasio, lead singer from the band Pfish, had taken Jerry's spot that night. Bruce Hornsby assumed keyboards, filling in for deceased Brent Mydland.

Fifty years. They had taken me to exotic places like the Mars Hotel, Franklin's Tower and Terrapin Station. They introduced me to women who could wade in a drop of dew while wearing scarlet begonias. They told stories of menacing dire wolves and mysterious lights across an evening sky. They helped me relate to the mythology of life and love—always encouraging me to "keep on truckin.'"

When the lights came on and the last encore note fell to earth, I hugged my brother and his wife and we high-fived. We wandered back across an expanse of green golf course and a thousand memories to our friends.

The car was unusually heavy with middle-age fatigue until someone whispered, "Man, that was awesome." It was indeed special to have been able to say thank you to my band of fifty years and to experience it with my brother and family—so many tangled roots in the living tree of my life. I kept thinking about the lyrics to so many songs written by Robert Hunter. It was a moment in time, a soft ripple in the water of entire generation that would expand into concentric circles for one night and slowly fade. We were stopping here for a moment along this "road between the dark and the light of dawn."

And it was all right.

Saint Michael's Letter to Millennials at Commencement

> " In life you make the small decisions with your
> head and the big decisions with your heart."
> —OMID KORDESTANI

A COUPLE OF years ago, English teacher David McCullough Jr. had the audacity to tell a group of seniors from Wellesley High School in Massachusetts that they were not special at all, even though he had given some of them passing grades in his class.

"Contrary to what your U9 soccer trophy suggests," he said, "or your glowing seventh-grade report card, despite every assurance of a certain corpulent purple dinosaur, that nice Mister Rogers, and your batty Aunt Sylvia, no matter how often your maternal caped crusader has swooped in to save you...you're nothing special."

Mr. McCullough went on to frame your demographic reality in stark terms. "So think about this: even if you're one in a million, on a planet of 6.8 billion that means there are nearly 7,000 people just like you."

Actually, that's 6,800 people, which slightly improves your odds. He also did not mention that at least half of those sleep with a goat at night.

Now some of you are thinking, "I never professed to be anything special and it's been hours since I have tweeted anything profound. GTFO, dude!" On the other hand, some of you might be elated to think that you have 7,000 twins running around and years from now you'll try to pull together all your changelings for a rave on some South Pacific atoll.

What Mr. McCullough was saying has been on the mind of an entire generation of parents who are now a tad worried about how they have raised their beloved children. Our greatest fear is that we have loved you so much we have not prepared you for your first fistfight with someone who has less to lose than you do. While you exude self-confidence, we wonder if we are preparing Pickett at Gettysburg or the Custer at Little Big Horn. Are we pumping you up with illusory élan or are we infusing you with an energy that will sustain you during the inevitable tough days that lie ahead?

You are part of a demographic cohort called Millennials. Authors Strauss and Howe educated us that your tribe is characterized by extreme confidence, social tolerance, a strong sense of entitlement, and the narcissistic tendency to take photographs of yourself and post them a hundred times a day. Like the generations that preceded you, you are regularly accused of being pampered and unprepared. Yet, Strauss and Howe boldly predict that you will become civic-minded and in the face of some yet-to-be-defined crisis will emerge as a hero generation.

Of course you're cocky. Every generation feels superior to those that preceded it. With the benefit of hindsight, you can judge us more accurately than we can judge you. You have the facts to prove it. You can see every one of our generation's gaffes, miscues, political blunders, hypocrisies, and prescription medications.

When you were born, most of us read something by Malcolm Gladwell or an article in *Parents* magazine telling us that if we desired you to be high-performance outliers, we had to hold you back a grade. As a result, your graduating class is an uneven skyline of red-shirted college students and over-achieving youngsters. Some of you have been driving since your sophomore year—a few legally.

As your parents, we celebrated every one of your prosaic little accomplishments—and I mean every one. We attended more recitals, art shows, scrimmages, games, and microscopic milestones, not wanting to miss or regret a moment of your lives. We were and are your biggest fans. You taught us that material satisfaction has a brief shelf life, while true joy arises from seeing those you love get what they need.

You were pretty normal as small kids. Like all children, you loved the notion of having special powers. You read Harry Potter and got your first taste of dystopia in *The Hunger Games*. Up to that point, your idea of dystopia was a home without a pimped-out basement or any kind of "because-you-live-here" chores.

Our job always has been to love you until you learn to love yourself. If you don't believe us, it's in our position descriptions, which are filed down at City Hall.

It is also within our province to warn you that life is not all green lawns and Chinese take-out. Many of us grew up with parents who hit first and asked questions later. Everything was our fault. We had chores that paid less than minimum wage and had to do them before we could breathe.

Our fathers did not attend many of our scholastic events because they were off practicing their swearing and forehand spanking. Moms carried the load and still do, though dads are more involved, hit less, and only swear at MSNBC and Fox and after 11 p.m., when everyone else has gone to bed.

No matter how differently you have grown up, we know that you are just like we were—excited, clueless, capable of achieving great things and ready to commit momentous acts of stupidity. We like your style but it would reassure us if you would occasionally look up from your phones, if for no other reason than to see the bad guys when they are coming your way.

We see you seniors like Internet start-ups—full of promise and cool ideas, and with a market cap that far exceeds the fact that you still don't make any money. However, our irrational exuberance for you keeps us investing.

Please understand we do not like regulating your every move as teenagers, but we are now being told that it is our fault if you screw up. Here's the news: it isn't.

Life is messy, like your bathroom. You will fail—all by yourself, and it will seem weird the first time you don't immediately hear that familiar whump-whump of the parental helicopter on the horizon. You'll have your Ramadi moments—isolated, with no air support, and surrounded by circumstances that trigger all your self-centered fears. It's in these moments you will find your capacity to dig in and fight harder. You'll appreciate everything you truly earn more than what is given to you.

Failure is painful, but it is not the end of life. As your revered principal has always told you, every door is open to you from this point. It's only by making the wrong choices that you close a door.

However, if you do, you can recover. America loves a comeback. Just ask Bill Clinton, who is the only head of state in U.S. history to generate successive budget surpluses, be unsuccessfully impeached, have an affair, stay married, be president, and possibly become the first First Gentleman.

In life, as in nature, the seeds of true character germinate only during the wet winters of personal crisis. Clean streets don't immunize you from life. Some of you already have felt the sting of broken homes and tragedy. Most of you handled your challenges with incredible grace. Through these tough times, you guys cared for and loved each other. That capacity to put someone or something ahead of you is a sign of great emotional intelligence.

Keep it up. Lift your eyes from your screens and continue to focus on other people because, as a rule of thumb, most of you are your own worst enemies.

And because every commencement address must have some pithy advice, here's mine:

- If you're going to college, don't waste the next four years. Get your butt out of bed and go to class. It costs about $2,230 per class, so show up and learn something. There's more to life than knowing how to make a mean Mai Tai. To succeed today, you'll need the equilibrium of a jet pilot and the guts of a burglar. You acquire those skills in alleyways, not in your room watching six consecutive seasons of *Breaking Bad*.
- If your first roommate is nicknamed "Lysol" or "Candyman," ask for a new one. The semester won't end well.
- Never sign up for a class that meets before 11 a.m.

- Remember that people are not FTEs or headcount; we are all souls on a spiritual journey. Everyone has value.
- Be a rock of predictability and an oasis of empathy.
- Never take the last of anything.
- Make your bed when you stay at someone's house and strip the sheets when you leave.
- Don't wear shoes without socks.
- Make a gratitude list every day and learn how to delay your own gratification.
- Find a hero.
- Don't be a victim. I assure you that whatever higher power you worship has the same desire for you that we do—for you to be happy and to leave the world a better place than you found it.
- Remember Rome was not built in a day and it rotted from within because of weak politicians, foreign wars, and the fact that everyone was inside with their iPods on and couldn't hear the Vandals coming. For that reason alone, always keep a window open.
- Also remember you are today's special, but every day the menu changes. Stay strong, have fun, but don't ruin your chances for public office at your first college party. We need someone in Congress who will be looking out for us when we are wandering around town looking for our missing bag of string.
- Don't be afraid. We are all souls moving along a human continuum that is at one end anchored by ignorance, self-worship, and tanning salons, and on the other side by love and humility. Think any Kardashian at one extreme and Mother Theresa on the other. We each rise and fall along this silk thread of free will called life. Many of the mistakes we make stem from a self-centered fear of rejection, fear of not getting what we believe we need, fear of fear, and fear of not having at least three gigs on our cell phone or personal computer.
- Don't watch MSNBC or Fox; you'll live longer. *South Park* is okay.
- Be kind. Say "I'm sorry" and mean it.

- Learn to compete. Everyone doesn't always get a trophy. You will be knowledge workers who compete with two billion peers who believe it is time for you to wait on their tables and rake their leaves. The shelf life of your knowledge in a digital age is perishable, which means you must keep learning forever. Most of those competing with you did not spend last night watching *True Detective*, texting and tweeting, or mixing Red Bulls and vodka. They were studying math, engineering, finance, and science and actually liking it. Your faceless competitors are intellectually hungry, well trained, and eat fewer calories in a day than many of you eat in a meal.

- Look for ways to serve others, even those with whom you compete. In losing yourself in service, you will become a person who is more beautiful and capable than your wildest imagination could have dreamed.

- Smile and say hello to everyone. People matter and their lives matter. Don't allow yourself to dehumanize anyone. Every man's, woman's, or child's death diminishes you, whether it is in Danbury or Darfur. Learn the names of the people who pick up your trash, serve your food, drive your bus, clean your living areas, collect your tolls, and serve your community.

- Do not borrow class notes from anyone who watches reruns of *Jersey Shore* or has suffered more than three concussions.

- Travel. We are three hundred million Americans on a planet of six billion people. Do not be one of the 92 percent of Americans who do not possess a passport and have never traveled beyond the border. Don't apologize for being an American. Don't think less of your country, just think of it less often when you're abroad.

- Seek to understand before being understood.

- Study the teachings of all the great prophets.

- Visit Arlington National Cemetery and never lose respect for our military.

- Go to John Lennon's grave and never lose respect for peacemakers.

- Never French kiss a cannibal.

- Use Purell often.

- Be careful what you wish for. Pray for courage and wisdom to effectively play the cards you are dealt and don't whine about getting a poor hand; you can always bluff.
- Sleep under the stars, but use a mosquito net.
- Never try to outrun the police in a Ford Granada or give a ride to a hitchhiker with a prosthetic hook.
- Don't party too hard; all you are doing is medicating your ability to live life. Flume, Kanye, and Dave Matthews sound just as good without losing control, and you are much more likely to sing on key.
- Exercise regularly. The "freshman 20" is real!
- Don't feel sorry for yourself. It's a waste of time. Your best lessons will come in the form of pain: physical, emotional, intellectual, and psychic. Although these moments of clarity are difficult, you are getting exactly what you need (which may be quite different from what you want). There will be days when it seems like the entire cosmos has turned its back on you. Remember that you are only given what you can handle and strife is the ultimate compliment from a God who has a wicked curveball and a highly evolved sense of humor. As you struggle with these trials, you will discover a lot about yourself and others, including who your real friends are and who was only hanging around for the free food.
- Learn to forgive. Resentment is junk food. It creates emotional fat and has no value. I have to admit vindictiveness tastes good but it ends up giving you heartburn. Pray for your enemies.
- Risk rejection, knowing that somewhere out there, someone beyond your wildest expectations is waiting to be your partner. You just may have to travel through Slovenia to meet them.
- Don't get depressed about the way you find the world. Your job is to change it and our job is to try to stay out of your way while you pull down some of our grand monuments to self-interest.
- Don't blindly accept a two-party system.
- Crank the music but invite your neighbors to the party so they don't call the police.

- Write thank-you notes.
- Do something nice for someone every day but don't tell a soul. You will know what you did and 365 acts of kindness later, you will be changed for the better.

Each of you is a candle in the dark—a catalyst for change wherever you go. You do not have to travel to the edges of the globe to find the marginalized, the underserved, the hopeless and the inhumane. You just have to get out of your self-interest long enough to notice the need.

I'll end up where I started: with your parents. Always remember that we were once young, too. We were so much cooler than you think, but we are not allowed to tell you our stories as it violates the terms of our parole.

I hope you will live well and remember de Tocqueville's famous line: "When the past no longer illuminates the future, the spirit walks in darkness."

Good luck.

About the Author

MICHAEL TURPIN IS a graduate of literature from Claremont McKenna College and is a native of San Marino, California. He has lived in Los Angeles, San Francisco, London, and New York. A healthcare consultant by day, he indulges his passion for writing as a contributing columnist for magazines, newspapers, and a popular blog that covers a range of topics from popular culture to the travails of modern-day parents. He draws heavily on his generation's life experiences and his literary heroes—Erma Bombeck, Woody Allen, David Sedaris, and Bill Bryson—to remind readers that the only normal people we know are those who choose to close their curtains at night. This is his third book. His first two novels, T-Rex By the Tail and Bicentennial Rex, are humorous anthems to the alpha fathers and pragmatic mothers of the Silent Generation and the passing of an age known as "Jurassic" parenting. Turpin lives in New Canaan, Connecticut, with his wife and three teenaged children.

Made in the USA
San Bernardino, CA
02 November 2015